RETHINKING CONGREGATIONAL DEVELOPMENT

George E. Morris, Editor

Nine church leaders speak out on the revitalization of existing congregations and the development of new ones.

Prepared under the direction of the Institute for World Evangelism—the World Methodist Council. Book three in the World Evangelism Library.

Discipleship Resources   Nashville

Library of Congress Catalog Card Number: 84-71366

ISBN: 0-88177-012-4

Contents

Foreword. . . . . *W. James Cowell* vi

Introduction . . . . *George E. Morris* vii

Chapter 1. . . . . *Earl D. C. Brewer* 1
Re-visioning Congregational Development

Chapter 2 . . . . *Ezra Earl Jones* 13
Analysis/Overview
of New Church Development

Chapter 3 . . . . *George E. Morris* 20
Theological Bases
for Congregational Development

Chapter 4 . . . . *Luther E. Smith, Jr.* 34
The Vital Congregation:
Socio-Cultural Factors

Chapter 5 . . . . *Robert L. Wilson* 44
The Nature and Function of the Parish
in a Changing World

Chapter 6. . . . . *René O. Bideaux* 55
Our Missional Constituencies:
Unchurched, Unconnected, and Unknown

Chapter 7 . . . . *Gordon Bruce Turner* 65
On the Outside Looking in:
The Story of the Church Dropout and What the
Church Can Do about It

Chapter 8. . . . . *James R. Maxfield* 81
New Congregations:
A Mission and in Mission

Chapter 9 . . . . *Kennon L. Callahan* 86
Looking to the Future:
Foundational Principles for
Congregational Development

To Phoebe Wang Lee,
whose commitment to evangelism has been a constant
source of encouragement to all who work with the
Institute for World Evangelism.

Foreword

It was my privilege to attend the consultation on "Rethinking Congregational Development" in Atlanta shortly after assuming my present position with the Board of Discipleship of The United Methodist Church. The presentations provided background information necessary to understand where we are in congregational development in North America and sufficient challenge to move beyond "brick and mortar" concerns in church extension and redevelopment to actually focusing on the real objective of our mission—unchurched and hurting people everywhere. The consultation reinforced my belief that the beginning point in new church development is not buildings, sites, money, but people! The sessions stimulated my thinking regarding the biblical foundations for what we are about, in and through the gathered church.

It is my hope that others reading this volume will gain insight and renewed enthusiasm for the task of congregational development and be better equipped to assist new and long-established churches in becoming effective centers of Christian mission. Only as churches reach out to persons, receive them into the membership and fellowship circle of congregations, help to relate them to God and develop them as disciples, and send them forth in mission and ministry to make their communities more loving and just, can they fulfill the task that beckons.

I am indebted to the Institute for World Evangelism of the World Methodist Council, the Candler School of Theology, Emory University, various denominational agencies, and personally to George Morris for coordinating *Rethinking Congregational Development* for my growth and reflection. May you be challenged in a similar manner through this volume.

W. James Cowell, Director
Congregational Development
Board of Discipleship
The United Methodist Church

Introduction

Perhaps over 100 million people in North America do not claim an allegiance to any Christian group. To get this in perspective, we must realize there are only six nations in the world that have a total population larger than that figure. North America is one of the most fertile mission fields in the world. The need for the development of new congregations and the revitalization of existing ones is undeniable and urgent.

What kind of strategy must be followed if we are to meet the challenge of reaching these unchurched millions? Part of the strategy is based on the principle that new churches are started through the ministry of older established ones. Therefore, one good way to learn how to build new churches is to learn how to make existing churches new. We know that larger and larger numbers of unchurched people continue to live in the vicinity of existing churches. Enhancing the church where it already exists is indispensable to the task of missional outreach.

Another part of an overall strategy acknowledges the fact that a large percentage of our North American population will continue to be unchurched if we depend solely on existing churches. Throughout the history of the Christian movement the development of new congregations has been a primary means of evangelizing. The failure to develop new congregations has contributed largely to the massive membership losses of our denominations. New congregations must be developed in order for great numbers of unchurched persons to be brought to faith in Jesus Christ and responsible membership in the church. Moreover, as a consequence of the development of new congregations, we will begin to see the revitalization of those existing churches that sieze new congregational development as a part of their missional mandate.

Underlying both parts of this overall strategy is the absolute necessity of finding ways to enable the people in the Wesleyan tradition to overcome their "four-walls mentality" and become, once again, a powerful evangelistic and missional movement in North America.

It was in response to these urgent needs that the Institute for World Evangelism at Candler School of Theology sponsored a major North American Consultation entitled "Rethinking Congregational Development." This Consultation brought together one hundred delegates from Canada, Mexico, and the United States. For five days and nights the delegates participated in plenary sessions, panel discussions, workshops, and Wesley class meetings. Together with an outstanding cadre of leaders, they wrestled with a wide range of challenges and issues regarding the revitalization of existing congregations and the development of new ones.

The material in this book comprises the major addresses given at the Consultation. I wish to thank each contributor. Together we share this material with the prayer that it may help to launch a major new thrust in congregational development. Perhaps this book will help to sensitize us and enable us to hear what the Spirit is saying to the churches.

George E. Morris, Director
The Institute for World Evangelism
Candler School of Theology

Chapter 1

Re-visioning Congregational Development

Earl D. C. Brewer

It would seem to be the hope of denominations within the Wesleyan tradition to launch a new emphasis on congregational development and redevelopment. This may be easier said than done. Our sayings may be within conventional wisdom and our doings within customary practice. If so, our faith will continue to falter and our work to weaken.

Let us question whether this new emphasis is going to be modeled after a clergy meeting of the Church of England in the eighteenth century or after a meeting of Wesley and his followers in the streets and in house class meetings. The outcome is yet to be determined, but it will probably not be with Wesley. In earlier days the Wesleyan Movement was characterized by spiritually motivated hearts with new visions and new ways of moving toward those visions. What does all this say to us? Is the Spirit still flowing in modern Wesleyan structures or does God seek other channels? Are the Methodist bureaucratic arteries so clogged with satisfaction over the status quo that Wesleyan hearts beat sluggishly without the aerobic quickening of the Holy Spirit? Do we face the challenge of this new emphasis with warmed-over visions and rearranged strategies of years gone by? Or are we prepared for a prayerful and powerful Wesleyan paradigm shift, toward visions of a new earth, a new people, and a new church with a new mission?

Surely our dream is for a modern-day Aldersgate and post-Aldersgate experience of fired-up hearts, obsessive visions, and saving grace. Since most of our heads are already full of visions, perhaps *re-visioning* is a more appropriate word. It is not so much that we re-vision for others, but that we do it together. With this in mind, a design for visioning is included. You may use it for note-taking as a holistic frame for visioning.

This approach to vision is grounded in the human capacity to transcend ourselves and to move forward. It is rooted in our being created in the image of a transcendent God. Looking at the design,

1

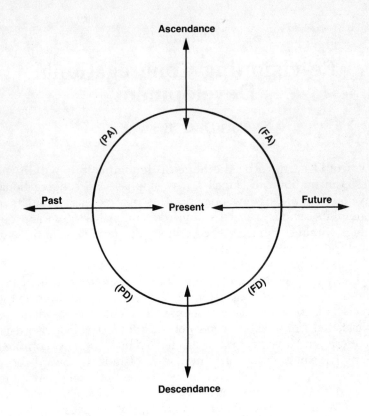

Ascendance

(PA)   (FA)

Past   Present   Future

(PD)   (FD)

Descendance

temporal transcendence (past-present-future) is represented by the horizontal lines across the middle of the circle. Transcendence of quality (good-bad, angelic-demonic, heaven-hell, life-death, crucifixion-resurrection, positive-negative) is represented by the vertical lines. Ascendance is considered positive and descendance negative. This may be called spatial transcendence.

The development of a vision, like all of life, is done in the present. This temporal dimension is seen in the circle. Words or phrases placed in the upper half of the circle are considered ascendant or positive, and those in the lower half descendant or negative. The quadrants surrounding the circle may be used for notes on your visioning. To the left are quadrants dealing with the past, and to the right those of the future. Combining the temporal and spatial aspects of transcendence, the southwest quadrant (PD) represents the past and the descendant, the northwest (PA) the past-ascendant, the northeast (FA) the future-ascendant, and the southeast (FD) the future-descendant. The design sheet and these details are provided to indicate that holistic visioning involves both temporal and spatial transcendence, and both positive and negative elements. Let us now move to its use in re-visioning congregational development.

All visioning is done in the present, drawing on the past and creating images of the future. In the upper or positive half of the circle, there is space for tremendous optimism. In North America, denominations within the Wesleyan tradition currently claim nearly 60,000 congregations and upwards of 15 million members in the United States. One denomination, The United Methodist Church, contains the largest number of churches and members, but three other denominations (the African Methodist Episcopal with around two million; the African Methodist Episcopal, Zion, with over one million; and the Christian Methodist Episcopal with nearly 800,000 members) contribute largely to the total membership. Jointly they have around 14,000 congregations. Smaller bodies also provide resources for future congregational development. In Mexico, five bodies report over 60,000 members and in Canada five denominations claim under one million members. These bodies have considerable financial resources, trained clergy, and dedicated laity.

These and other positive indicators of the present are matched by unequalled opportunities. There are more unchurched people in North America than ever before. It is difficult to reach agreement on ways of counting the nonchurched. However, using the methods of the Glenmary Research Center's 1980 *Churches and Church Membership*, somewhere between 40 and 50 percent of the U.S. population is not counted in the membership of religious bodies. This translates into around 100 million persons. These proportions probably apply to Mexico and Canada as well. Clearly, the fields have never been riper for harvest, and the resources for evangelism have never been greater than the present. The Holy Spirit seems willing to join need and opportunity in a great outburst of evangelism and congregational development during the years between now and the end of this century.

Yet the present also presents some hindrances. Let's note some of these in the lower half of the circle. The United Methodist Church is the only Methodist body losing both membership and congregations. Obviously, such negative trends must be reversed. The other Methodist bodies registered gains in both membership and congregations during the past two decades. All the Methodist family members in the United States and Canada gained about 1 percent in churches and membership while the population was growing around 25 percent in the United States, and 34 percent in Canada. In Mexico the gain in Methodist membership was around 70 percent, while the population nearly doubled over the past 20 years. In all of North America, Methodism is becoming a smaller and smaller proportion of the population.

These data indicate a bare maintenance level, with United Methodism even falling below that, and Mexican Methodism rising above it. Are the people called Methodists willing to settle, like the Church of England of Wesley's day, for ministries of maintenance in the midst of significant changes and opportunities? If the answer is yes, the contents of this book will fall on deaf ears. But if the answer is maybe, maybe not, or a resounding no, the people called Methodists have their work cut out for them. It is easy to cultivate routine ministries for the maintenance of prestige, power, privilege, tradition, money, status quo, church structures, and procedures, while not caring about the unchurched, and accommodating to social injustices and evils in the world around us. It is difficult to break out of ecclesiastical molds into missional and evangelistic outreach ministries to and with millions who are poor in spirit, body, and resources for living—people who are faced with injustice and oppression.

Now it is true that both the "holding-in-place" ministries of maintenance and the "breakthrough" ministries of mission must go on. It is the balance between them that is important. Whenever and wherever maintenance exceeds mission, as at present, the body is in trouble.

If a picture of the present situation shows lights and shadows on our prospects for the future, what about our past? The northeast quadrant of the diagram is the place to make notes on the ascendant or positive past. The remarkable historical fact about Methodism in this country was its evangelistic outreach and its planting of preaching places. The Wesleyan spirit, discipline, and organizational style produced astonishing results on the frontier. Often before a county was formed, a Methodist circuit was established; a Methodist annual conference often preceded statehood. This evangelistic fervor extended to slaves in the South and to free blacks in the North. The organization of the African Methodist Episcopal Church; the African Methodist Episcopal Church, Zion; and the Colored Methodist Church (now, the Christian Methodist Episcopal Church)

4

aided in this process. Other groups split off from the parent body over issues of doctrine or administration, and several of them (e.g., the Methodist Protestant Church) grew to considerable size. Prior to the Civil War, the Methodist Episcopal Church split along North-South lines over the issue of slavery.

The Civil War was a watershed for Methodism as it was for so much of history in the United States. Methodism had increased in membership from around 2 percent of the population in 1800 to around 6 percent by 1870. If that evangelistic rate had continued during the second one hundred years, Methodism would report around 23 million members today, 10 million more than current records show. The data for Canada doubtless reflect a smiliar experience during the frontier, as well as the slow-down in recent times. Clearly, Mexico is still in an evangelistic upswing.

For answers to these perplexing data, let's look at the negative or descendant southwestern quadrant in the diagram. Some unhappy notes need to be sounded. After the Civil War, immigration shifted from Protestant England and Northern Europe to Catholic Central and Southern Europe. Methodism was unable to break out of its English language and cultural background to cope successfully with the pluralistic immigration.

The frontier eventually gave way to urbanization. Methodism had adopted Wesley's patterns for the frontier but found itself at a loss to shift gears into an equally effective urban strategy. This is reflected today in the fact that the larger the city, the smaller the proportion of Methodist members within it. Yet, there are counties with rural and small town populations where every fifth person is a Methodist.

In spite of Wesley's stand on slavery, Methodism in this country compromised on the issue. White racism has been practiced across the years and into the present. One result has been the formation of black Methodist churches. Blacks today make up nearly one-third of all Methodist members in the United States, but only a little more than a tenth of the population. This fact should not be lost when we think of congregtional development or evangelistic outreach.

The frontier mentality of Methodism was helpful during the first hundred years but hurtful during the second hundred. We are the only episcopal form of church government with a mandatory annual appointment of ministers. This yields dysfunctionally short tenures for clergy. In many situations, especially in smaller parishes, pastors hardly get acquainted with and accepted by members before they move elsewhere. Short-term planning or no planning at all is not

5

conducive to nurture and "inreach," to say nothing of mission and outreach.

The doctrine of general ministry states that any minister can serve anywhere. This may have fitted the frontier, but it is a limiting factor in today's complex world. Now and then, a young seminary graduate is appointed to a vacant lot to develop a congregation, usually with no training along this line, and a few years later is appointed to an established parish. That method of planting a church leaves much to be desired.

What has just been said about congregational development during the second hundred years, with a few exceptions, such as after World Wars I and II, can be said with even more force about missional outreach through evangelism. Since many congregations are growing slowly, are stagnant or declining, the need for the revitalization of existing congregations is urgent. To my knowledge, there are few programs in theological education or in the plans of general or annual conference agencies to undergird such an emphasis. We need to re-learn how to extend Methodist membership through existing congregations.

The highly touted connectionalism of Methodism seems under strain both vertically and horizontally. Many congregations feel on the margin of general and annual conference agencies. The limited up-down flow is channeled largely through the district and the down-up contacts are primarily financial. To put it in the words of a layperson in a small membership church, "We get a preacher and we pay the apportionments." Of course, much more flows up and down vertical connectionalism, but it is often lost both ways in the transmission. Surely, the Holy Spirit is working to unclog these sluggish connectional pipelines.

In the early 1800s the average number of members served on a circuit was around four hundred. Today the average size pastoral charge in United Methodism remains around four hundred. In other Methodist bodies it is probably less. Early ministers covered many miles on horseback, organized preaching places and class meetings in homes, brush arbors, and open air. The minister and a few assistants looked after the spiritual welfare of as many members as do modern ministers. Most pastors today serve fewer than four hundred members, mostly in one congregation. They have cars, telephones, radios, televisions, duplicating machines, and other means of transportation and communication. What if they were also captured by the spiritual and practical vision of the early circuit riders? If so, our annual conferences could begin and end in a glorious celebration like unto many of the early annual conferences.

Horizontally, congregations across Methodism have lost effective missional contact with their communities. Inner-city churches with thousands of people nearby are losing members, some by substantial numbers. Some of these are in transitional communities with changes in race or class. Often human need and social injustice abound, but many local pastors and members wash their hands of the conditions and changes, and withdraw to celebrate the past. Too often they are satisifed with the status quo, and fail in their missional outreach. Horizontal connectionalism largely fails also in relating one Methodist congregation to another in common mission within the community. This applies within a single Methodist denomination and even more so across denominations within the Methodist family. Congregations connecting with congregations of other denominations is rare indeed. Congregational individualism and the rootlessness of denominational agencies have tended to push Methodist connectionalism into ineffectiveness in mission.

In recent years, Methodist seminaries have tended to focus on education for a professional ministry largely within the four walls of the church. This is preparation for "safe" ministries within sanctioned structures, such as preaching, worship, pastoral care, and Christian education. Little attention is given to ministries beyond the four walls, to say nothing of congregations without walls. With rare exceptions there would seem to be little encouragement, much less definite theological programs, for the training of spirit ministers, those with hearts aflame by the Holy Spirit to participate in breakthrough ministries of outreach and mission. Wesley had to go outside the Church of England to respond evangelistically and organizationally to the urgings of his heart warmed by the Holy Spirit to minister to displaced and uprooted workers caught in the early stages of the Industrial Revolution. What about us in the early days of the post-industrial society?

Other pictures, both beautiful and bleak, could be drawn from our past. May these incomplete sketches impel us to go to our own private or agency canvas and draw in the learnings and concerns, both positive and negative, for future congregational development and revitalization within the context of the community and our society.

It is to visions of possible futures that we now turn. Let's look at the southwest (FD) quadrant, reflecting the future as descendant or negative. This can be painted in with a few bold strokes. The blunt truth is that unless there are massive intervention strategies of the Spirit, the trends for Methodism in North America will continue downward. The recent rate of membership growth for Methodism in Mexico, Canada, and the black denominations in the United States, although on the plus side, were far below population increases. Add to this the actual decline in members and congregations for The United Methodist Church, and the total picture is not optimistic. Indeed, United Methodism, if it continues losing at the same rate as over the last twenty years, will claim only 2.57 percent of the population in the year 2000. This would be about the same as in 1810.

The negative trends flowing out of our past, some of which have already been mentioned, can greatly hinder our mission as Methodists in the years to come. Unless we can be self-critical and spirit-led, the future may seem more like that depicted by the four horsemen of the apocalyptic Revelation (6:1-8) than that of the visionary and tireless circuit riders of the American frontier. We need to be careful in celebrating our past lest we celebrate the hindrances which must be removed if our future is to be other than continual descendance.

Finally, let us look to the northeast quadrant of ascendant futures. What is the Spirit saying to Methodists about positive and hopeful images of the future? Let us follow the leadership of the Spirit in our own visioning. Here are some hints, hopefully growing out of the yearnings of the Spirit.

The Spirit is saying to us that "business as usual" is not good enough to be about God's business in the future. From the smallest membership congregation to the highest authorities, there goes out a call for contrition and confession over our lukewarm and limited commitments, our playing it safe and our unwillingness to take risks. The Spirit is leading us away from a continuing scenario of descendance toward a transforming scenario of ascendance and resurrection. We need to crucify, or have crucified for us, all those conditions, structures, powers, customs, and traditions which have been golden calves enticing us into secular idolatry and spiritual indifference. We need to resurrect, or have resurrected for us, the burning heart, the spiritual quest, the love and concern for all people everywhere, especially those most unlike us. We need a total commitment to being and becoming the Body of Christ and doing the bidding of Christ in the world. Herein move the spiritual ener-

8

gies of agony and ecstasy between the cross and the empty tomb. We may, indeed, be too blind and dull, too satisfied and secure to risk walks along modern Emmaus roads where our spirits may be stirred and human needs exposed. Unless we are willing to undergo radical spiritual surgery and transformation as persons and as denominations, little is likely to change in new or old congregations in the future.

Another part of the image for the future deals with the question, "Congregational development or revitalization to what end?" Are we primarily concerned with increasing membership or are we really committed to extending the Body of Christ and expanding Christ's mission in the world? Is the salvation of souls and societies our biblical goal or simply the enhancement of our bureaucracies? Constructive theological work needs to be done on the nature of congregations and their mission to persons and social structures.

If present congregations become spiritual centers of salvation and mission, they could serve as models for new ones. The process of renovating congregations should be aimed at the underchurched first, and the unchurched next. The underchurched are those members who participate marginally in faith development, attendance, and financial support. Their numbers may range from one-third to two-thirds of individual congregations. Generally, the smaller the membership, the smaller the proportion of the underchurched. Ministries to reduce the number of the underchurched and to spiritually nurture the overchurched would be aspects of spiritual revitalization. Redeveloped congregations would naturally reach out in evangelism and mission to the unchurched. If we cannot be in mission to the spiritual and social need of the unchurched in and through resurrected existing congregations, there is little hope that we can be successful through new congregations.

Yet a part of a hopeful future for Methodism is in planting new congregations in order to reach unchurched peoples and to engage in ministries to and with them. Who are these 100 million-and-more people of God outside the pastures of God? According to Hale's recent study (J. Russell Hale, *Who Are the Unchurched?* Washington: Glenmary Research Center, 1977), they may be placed in several categories: anti-institutionalists, boxed-ins, burned-outs, cop-outs, happy hedonists, locked-outs, nomads, pilgrims, publicans, the scandalized, true unbelievers, and the uncertain. How many of these unchurched are middle or lower class, affluent or in poverty, mainstreamers or marginals, oppressors or oppressed, children or

9

elderly, heterosexuals or homosexuals, undernourished in body or in soul? How many of these unchurched, regardless of similarities or differences, can be drawn into new or revitalized congregations?

A transformed scenario of the congregation in this coming communications age might include several features. There would be less emphasis on the size of the building and more on its utility. The sanctuary would be small and circular with the altar in the center. Services would be informal, celebrative, and focused on issues and mission of the group at worship. Group sharing, fellowship, Bible reading, prayer, planning, singing, liturgy, and common meals would close with the Lord's Meal. There would be several of these groups at worship and work throughout Sunday and during the week. Thus, religious services would be an everyday affair and not just Sunday occasions. The kitchen and meals together, including those without food, would take on new significance. In one room there would be banks of telephones, handled by volunteers on a twenty-four-hour basis to keep in touch with members, prospective members, and community persons in leadership or in need. Another room would have several computers with instant access to information about the members, the community, the church at large, and the world. These would be run by volunteers and used in various ministries of transformation. Another room would be equipped to receive and produce radio and television programs and to link various groups in the church and community and around the world through satellites, teleconferencing, and two-way cable communications. Much of the volunteer service could be done at the homes of the volunteers in contact with others. The cathedral church would be one with extensive communication capabilities to serve smaller groups over a wide area. The notion of congregations planted on a transportation basis (within walking distance and, then, within car-driving distance) would give way to congregations developed on a communications basis. The implications of this sketchy scenario for congregational development might be profound for the near and, especially, for the far future. Since the information-based age is upon us, existing congregations could revitalize themselves by moving in these directions. In these ways, information technologies would be put to use in communicating the good news of God to people.

It may be that the Spirit is speaking to us today through Wesley's original statement of the purpose of the people called Methodists, "not to form any new sect; but to reform the nation, particularly the church; and to spread scriptural holiness over the land" (*Wesley's Works*). Sects aplenty there are in the world, and they seem to be meeting the spiritual needs of people and growing, while the mainline churches are declining in numbers and in mission. The "powers and principalities" of the nation, and especially of the churches, have never been in greater need of transformation. The experience of scriptural holiness and its contagious spread to persons, congregations, and social structures remains a key goal of contemporary congregations.

Which of these words of the Spirit in Revelation 2:8-22 are appropriate for us today? To the church at Ephesus: "Fortitude you have but you have lost your early love. Think from what height you have fallen; repent and do as you once did." To the church at Smyrna: "Only be faithful till death, and I will give you the crown of life." To the church at Pergamum: "You are holding fast to my cause." To the church at Thyatira: "I know all your ways, your love and faithfulness, your good service and your fortitude; and of late you have done even better than at first." To the church at Sardis: "Though you have a name for being alive, you are dead. Wake up, and put some strength into what is left, which must otherwise die! For I have not found any work of yours completed in the eyes of my God." To the church at Philadelphia: "Look, I have set before you an open door, which no one can shut." To the church at Laodicea: "I know your ways; you are neither hot nor cold. How I wish you were either hot or cold. But because you are lukewarm, neither hot nor cold, I will spit you out of my mouth. You say, 'How rich I am! And how well I have done! I have everything I want in the world.' In fact, though you do not know it, you are the most pitiful wretch, poor, blind, and naked." And John's message to each of these churches, and to us today, ends with the ringing words: "Hear, you who have ears to hear, what the Spirit says to the churches."

The words of Jesus recorded in Acts 1:8 constitute the ancient yet urgent commission which grows out of our efforts to re-vision congregational development: "You shall receive power when the Holy Spirit has come upon you; and you shall be my witnesses in Jerusalem, and in all Judea and Samaria and to the end of the earth." This sets our sights. Congregations are to witness to those within their own membership (Jerusalem), then to those like themselves in the community (Judea), then to those unlike themselves (Samaria) and finally, to all the people of God around the globe.

Under the leadership of the heartwarming Spirit, our task is no less than to amplify and vivify this vision, to call Methodists every-where to Spirit-filled commitment to this commission, to update the ministries and means of transforming grace, to identify where and when God is at work in the world and join God there, to feel the fullness and immediacy of time for this venture as well as the long pull of decades and centuries, to arouse the financial support from the sleeping coffers of the church, to join hands with all Methodists, and to be frank enough to confess faults and failures and faithful enough to celebrate successes—all under the witness of the Holy Spirit with our spirits that we are God's and doing God's work in the world.

What seems clearly envisioned in the future of congregational development and revitalization is a massive spiritual and strategic paradigm shift of the magnitude of Wesley's in the eighteenth century. Such a shift would envision a whole world parish with a new sense of mission to all God's people on earth regardless of nationality, race, ideology, sex, class, or level of spiritual and phys-ical need. There would be special ministries to the starving, the sick, the oppressed, the poor, and those victimized by war and injustice. This is an urgent global vision to which we could respond as Meth-odists two hundred years ago did in their day. Whether we as twentieth century Wesleyans are up to the challenge is an open question. The Spirit and the scriptures surely say yes. If so, who or what is to say no?

Chapter 2

An Analysis/Overview of New Church Development

Ezra Earl Jones

On June 19, 1983, Chris Wallace reported on Pope John Paul II's visit to Poland on NBC's Sunday Night News. At one point in the newscast he said, "It takes a lot more than mortar and bricks to build a church." He was referring to a church in Krakow, Poland. The Polish government had brought new industry into Krakow, including new housing for the workers. No provision, however, was made for a church. The government would not issue a permit for a church. A priest, however, set up a temporary shed from which to celebrate Mass in the open air. Services continued and the people persisted in seeking permission for a church building. Thirteen years after the people began those efforts for a new church, a building—a beautiful building—had been completed and Chris Wallace reported that the Pope would dedicate it on his June 1983 visit to Poland. "It takes a lot more than mortar and bricks to build a church." That statement means one thing in Poland and another in North America where it is, nevertheless, just as true.

In 1947 a baby was born to a couple in a small village in West Kenya near the Ugandan border. The child grew, but at the age of six his father died. His mother kept him in school. At the age of fifteen, in 1962, a missionary came to his village and started a church. The missionary asked the boy if he would like to learn to read the Bible. He said that he would. When the missionary learned that the young man could already read and write, he said he would immediately enroll him in a mission school sixty miles away. The boy and his mother agreed that he should go. The congregation also agreed, but wanted the young man to return every weekend to teach them what he learned about the Bible. For three years, this young man left home early in the morning (3:00 A.M.) on Monday and retraced his steps back on Friday. Today, twenty years later, that small group of people in that small village have moved out to other villages and started other churches. Now there are 165 congregations representing 6,000 members in the villages of West Kenya. There are no bricks

13

and mortar, but there are 165 congregations! "It takes a lot more than mortar and bricks to build a church."

In the September 1982 issue of *Grapevine*, published by the Joint Stategy and Action Committee, James H. Davis described Methodist Church extension in the nineteenth century:

> When the Methodist Western Conference met in 1800, fifteen preachers were appointed to the entire Western country. For example, William Burke's circuit extended 100 miles each way in central Kentucky. Salaries were $64 per year. They lived off the land and the hospitality of the people.
>
> "The old itinerants went everywhere preaching," said an 1872 sermon to the Methodist Church Extension Society. "But as soon as they gathered a handful of converts, they organized them into a class. Then the next step was to build a chapel to give them a covering, a name, a character, and a notice that the church was to be a fixture in that neighborhood—a notice to the devil that his empire had been entered by a force that was there to fight him to the last."
>
> While the other denominations were building stately churches in the larger cities along the railroads, the Methodists were [calling people together] wherever there was a cluster of homes, expanding as rapidly as the frontier. In the five years 1866-1871, they erected more than 3,000 chapels and added more than 380,000 members. Simple and cheap, valued from $25 to $50, the chapel was erected by the people themselves.

Presbyterian researchers give five reasons why they did not grow as rapidly as the Methodists—how the Midwest was lost:

1. They insisted that missionaries had to be ordained and meet their educational requirements.

2. They waited until the population was adequate to support a full-time pastor.

3. Pressure for self-support tended to over-fund new developments.

4. Multiplying ecclesiastical machinery made the process cumbersome.

5. Some missionaries were sponsored by ecumenical mission organizations, so they did not know which denomination's church they were supposed to start.

In our heritage, it took "a lot more than mortar and bricks to build a church." A place of identification was important for the church—"a covering, a name, a character, and a notice to the devil . . . that the church was to be a fixture in the neighborhood." Bricks and mortar are important for any community institution, but it takes a lot more than mortar and bricks. To focus new church development on buildings is deadly.

Today, there is good news and bad news about new church development. The good news is that interest has not been greater in two decades in all mainline North American denominations. The bad news is that the pervasive image in people's minds when new churches are mentioned is of buildings and cost. Both in 1979 and 1983 in reporting on annual conferences in The United Methodist Church, *Newscope* noted high interest in new church development among the seventy-three annual conferences. Virtually all those references were to fund-raising and buildings rather than to the calling together of the people of God or about people who come seeking redemption.

The difference is between institutional concerns and evangelism concerns. Institutional concerns focus on preserving or extending the church. Evangelism focuses on people and their relationship to God. This confusion is the most significant characteristic of new church development today. There are several consequences of this confusion.

1. People are scared off by new church development specialists who report that it costs up to $500,000 to start a new church. One district superintendent recently told me that an NCD consultant estimated it would cost $800,000 to start a new church in a particular community within his district.

2. Some people quickly choose sides between what they perceive to be brick and mortar concerns on the one hand and mission concerns on the other. That is a false dichotomy and is not helpful.

3. We can and will start only a fraction of the number of churches that are needed because of the perceived high cost.

4. New churches concentrate too early in their existence on buildings to the detriment of gathering and nurturing people as a community.

5. The number of members a new church must recruit in its formative years to "justify" the financial investment is sometimes unrealistically high.

There are probably many reasons for the priority identification that we have with costs and buildings. The primary reason is that far too many of our new church development efforts are at conference, district, and other judicatory levels. Much of our effort is removed from the immediate needs of people in existing congregations to reach out to other people, to relate them to God, develop them as Christian disciples, and send them out to minister.

In 1976 I wrote a book (*Strategies for New Churches*, Harper and Row) about how to do new church development by concentrating the activities at the conference and district levels in The United Methodist Church and at similar judicatory levels in other denominations. I still believe that is important and that many new churches will be started without initiation by existing congregations. Today, however, I do not believe that should be the major way it is done. We are in danger of putting new wine in old wineskins, of taking the appropriate methods of the 1950s and 1960s and reusing them in the 1980s and 1990s when other methods may be better used.

I would like to offer my vision for new church development for the 1980s. I believe it will be one based on evangelism rather than on an institutional model. It is one focused on people rather than on costs and buildings. If we keep our eyes on the people, we will have no trouble finding the technology. If we focus on technology, we will lose the end for which our means are intended.

I suggest we do the following:

1. We must encourage existing local congregations to initiate new churches in nearby and far-away communities and support them in every way possible. This does not mean that existing congregations need to urge present members to join new congregations although, in some cases, some members may want to be a part of the new congregation. This should be seen as direct evangelism—people in one church reaching people who will become part of another congregation. Imagine what could happen in The United Methodist Church alone if each of the forty-five active bishops called together one dozen pastors and challenged them to a ministry of leading their people to start a new church in a new community. This in itself could yield more than 800 new congregations. If all the Methodist denominations in North America would adopt this goal, the number of new congregations would be multiplied again and again.

I believe that most pastors would be willing to adopt this if the expectation were laid before them.

2. We desperately need to train a core of pastors, particularly seminarians, in the unique task of starting a new congregation. With rare exceptions, that skill is not offered in our seminaries at present.

3. We must be willing to cross conference and judicatory lines in the creation of new congregations. In The United Methodist Church, the "connection" in new church development seems to work only through general agencies. We should have direct support and connections between conferences that need more new churches and those which have a wide view of evangelism and mission.

4. Let us not talk about buildings until after congregations are chartered, and let that talk be by church members instead of conference and judicatory leaders.

5. We must be willing to start new small churches. Currently, and in the past, we have refrained from starting churches which could not attain a membership of 300 members in three to five years. That is an unrealistic goal for many communities that need new churches. Let us start churches where they are needed, including communities that can only accommodate small ones.

6. Major effort needs to be expended in starting new churches through an extension of the Sunday school. This has been a major means throughout Methodist history and is still a major means in many parts of Latin America, Puerto Rico, and Hawaii, as well as other places. If we start new Sunday schools, many will develop into new churches. The others will continue as Sunday schools or may serve for a time before disbanding.

7. We have an opportunity to concentrate in our new church development efforts on immigrant groups. Methodism grew in this country because we were not particular about whom we would serve—that is, we did not direct our ministry only to certain nationality groups. We were willing to serve all who came. We planted churches to serve communities; some were homogenous, others heterogenous. We served whoever was there. We must do that again and we must focus our attention particularly on racial groups such as Asians and Hispanics who are coming into the United States in large numbers.

8. We must develop strategies for urban and rural areas as well as suburban areas. We have long known how to do general area surveys and strategies for suburban communities. Although we have

17

started some new churches in urban and rural areas in recent years, we have not developed adequate strategies apart from suburban strategies. We must do that.

9. Where necessary, we must be willing to start new congregations alongside existing congregations. Where existing congregations have difficulty reaching new community residents, we should start new Sunday schools or new churches for those people rather than lose them because of the inability of the existing congregation to attract them.

10. If we will let existing congregations who sponsor new churches, and the new churches themselves, directly pay the costs associated with developing new churches, we will be able to focus less of our attention on cost and more on the ministry of evangelism and mission—reaching out to people who need Christian community. People and churches who see new church development as evangelism have little difficulty finding the money for that purpose.

11. We should re-identify churches with communities. We should charter new congregations only when their identification with the community is clear. In recent years, there has been a tendency for churches to look for members wherever they may be found and to identify a church's community with the people who come. Historically, however, churches have been seen as part of a particular community (which may be as large as a metropolitan area or as small as one apartment complex). Failure to identify a church with a community leads to that church taking responsibility for serving only part of the people who live there.

12. Particularly in the early stages, we can use the laity and lay pastors, as well as fully ordained clergy, to initiate new churches. Training programs for lay people interested in evangelism and mission are much needed.

13. We must establish a reward system for churches and individuals who start new churches. On occasion, we do reward certain behaviors in the church. It would seem today that we do not reward behavior associated with new church development. We are here talking about the possibility of rewarding people involved in evangelism in which the results do not get registered on the rolls of their own congregations.

In 1977, New York City suffered its second blackout in twelve years due to power failure. In both blackouts of recent years in New York, the people found themselves frustrated in many ways—wondering through the night how they would be able to cope in the morning. One writer for the *New Yorker* magazine (July 25, 1977) told of walking in Central Park in the morning after the blackout. He said, "Several people on the park's pathways carried flashlights in their hands or in their back pockets. They seemed unwilling to let go of the sources of illumination that had served them through the night. Watching these well-to-do people carrying flashlights in the dazzling sunshine, we recalled the friend who had momentarily found himself thinking that the power failure had knocked out the sun. It seemed that New Yorkers everywhere were having a hard time sorting out which things in their lives were human-made and which were gifts of God."

The supreme gift of God is that "God is with us." That is what evangelism means—God is with us. Our task is to announce it, live it, and participate in it. That is the end of new church development. May God help us to keep our eyes on that end—to remember that "it takes a lot more than mortar and bricks to build a church," that our primary task is that of reaching out and receiving people as they are, helping to relate them to God, assisting in their development as Christian disciples, and sending them back into their communities to make them better places in which to live.

Chapter 3

Theological Bases for Congregational Development

George E. Morris

RATIONALE

Books on congregational development will ordinarily have at least a chapter devoted to theological emphases. Workshops, conferences, and consultations on congregational development, as a matter of course, will have a segment allocated to theological issues. That this should be the case needs no defense. But *why* we should, on what basis, and to what end, is by no means clear. As a result of this lack of clarity regarding rationale, the theological task is sometimes treated as an afterthought, or even worse, exploited as a means of giving ideological justification to go ahead with what we have already determined to do.

Consequently, I have elected to address the important question of *why* before moving on to the *what*. For our purposes, this seems to be the proper order lest we fall into the fatal trap suggested by T. S. Elliot who once said, "The last temptation is the greatest treason, to do the right deed for the wrong reason." Why is it necessary to give attention to theological bases?

First, I am convinced that the reason our methods of congregational development become haphazard and often abortive is the uncanny tendency to isolate our methods of programming from theological foundations. The church in North America is perennially being tempted to leap into techniques of congregational development and redevelopment without struggling with the whole process of establishing theological clarity. We are so oriented toward producing results that we become short-sighted when it comes to our theological task. Some leaders tend to get restless and impatient with tedious demands for theological clarity. They say, "Let's quit splitting theological hairs and get on with the business at hand." Thus, we plunge headlong into programming. We do our surveys and bring forth gigantic programs and emphases which grow up overnight like green bay trees. They sometimes die before our eyes

20

because they have nothing but printer's ink for sap and are stricken by a blight of sociological data.

Only as we face the tedium of theological reflection can we allow the parameters of the gospel to determine, regulate, and guide the parameters of our congregational development. Therefore, in the second place, we put emphasis on the theological perspective because we are mandated to center all that we do in the good news of Jesus Christ. Now this is not an attempt to disregard or belittle programs, surveys, or sociological studies. I merely wish to make the point that we do not start there. If the world writes our agenda, we should not be surprised to discover that we are preoccupied with the world's agenda! We simply must begin at the point of the gospel of Jesus Christ and view the task of congregational development in theological perspective. This means that all of our surveys, studies, programs, and methods are brought under the close scrutiny of the gospel. Moreover, our efforts are authentic only as they confirm the key events and perceptions in the gospel, and all our programs and methods must get their bearings from the gospel. We dare not reverse this process lest we distort the gospel and lead the church down a path filled with pitfalls and destined for frustration and failure. So our purpose must be to bring the gospel to bear on our understanding and implementation of congregational development.

Bringing the gospel to bear on the task of congregational development must not be confused with providing a theology *for* congregational development. Such an enterprise would tend to degenerate into something quite negative and irresponsible. It could encourage us to hammer out a coherent, rational, seemingly foolproof theological justification for what we have already determined to do. This way of doing theology is designed to justify an emphasis, a point of view, or a program of action. When we fall into this trap, our own agenda takes on an ultimacy it doesn't deserve, and we read the whole of Christian theology through the peephole of our particular program or agenda. In support of this, we attempt to reinterpret the whole of scripture on the basis of certain preferred texts. This robs theology of its self-critical function and reduces the theologian to a protagonist who lobbies for a particular point of view or program. As a consequence, theology is reduced to ideology. On the other hand, to bring the gospel to bear on congregational development means involving ourselves in a critical assessment—

21

allowing the light of the gospel to illumine, assess, and, where necessary, correct our plans and programs.

I am insisting that our programs for the development of new congregations and the redevelopment of existing ones must be given form and consciousness through the theological task, which contains, molds, and gives our programs vitality. When the world's agenda and our clever schemes become the final arbiter, this tends to dislocate the place of the good news of Jesus Christ. What gospel there is left falls prey to innumerable sweetenings and adaptations which denature Christianity by adjusting it to our world, our own plans, and our own devices. Ultimately, the Christian message loses its saltiness and becomes sugary.

In saying that theology grows out of the good news of Jesus Christ, and insisting that our agenda as Christians must be in line with the gospel, I am not insinuating that the gospel is a seamless garment of infallible, dogmatic answers to every programmatic question. This mistake has led to the reduction of the gospel to smooth doctrinal propositions or prescriptions which claim to embody the substance of salvation in dogmatics. But, the story of the gospel does not come to us all smooth and harmonized with no rough edges. We often overlook the fact that there are four Gospels in the New Testament, not just one. There is a James as well as a Paul, a rich variety of theological formulations taking shape in terms of radically different contexts and persons. For this inherent reason, the gospel isn't seen exactly the same by everyone. Every major Christian denomination has its own conception of the gospel and its own conception of how the Great Commission is fulfilled and how churches are to be developed or revitalized.

Having acknowledged this diversity, I am yet convinced of the normative role the gospel must play. Despite this dynamic diversity even in the New Testament writings, there is a commonality in terms of the apostolic witness of these early Christians. In the New Testament writings we find the church's urgent confession that God mediates the good news of redeeming love through Jesus Christ. And, in the Bible as a whole, we survey the story of God's revelation—a story which highlights the gathering of a people and the pilgrimage they take together.

Here I can only attempt a bare-bones outline of this revelation,[1] but attempt I must, for this revelation is the bedrock of all our theologizing and mission. From the beginning it must be acknowledged that God is the originator, initiator, source, and goal of this divine revelation. Therefore, it follows that the biblical and theological foundations of congregational development are deeply rooted in the nature of a creating, redeeming, and sanctifying God. Since God is central to the act and process of congregational development, it must be viewed from theological perspectives. If the action of God is central, how could it be otherwise? Let us rehearse the story of divine revelation.

I must tell the story from the Christian perspective. It must be acknowledged, however, that the heart of the Christian story is set within the broader context of a living tradition which recounts the history of God's dealings with the whole human family. Though the Christian story centers upon the event of Jesus Christ, it is clear that God's action in Christ does not stand alone. It cannot be properly understood without constant reference to the whole story of God's activity—past, present, and future. For the Christian, the event of God in Jesus Christ is the focusing center from which we view the deeper meaning of the whole story of God's dealings with the human family.

THE GOSPEL STORY

The Christian story is a story about God's vision of *shalom*. The Hebrew word *shalom* attempts to embody the biblical vision of God's central, full, and ultimate intention for all creation. "In the beginning" God had a vision of a world of peace, justice, freedom, hopefulness, and well-being. It was a vision consistent with God's own being. The unfolding of salvation history traces God's struggle to establish this reconciling peace, freedom, and hopefulness among humankind and with persons and nature. It is out of this vision that God created.

Persons were created in God's image and were intended to be the historic actors who live in and for God's vision of *shalom*. That is, being in God's image, human beings were created to be in relation to God and to one another, not in isolation. Reflecting the relational nature of God, humans were created as relational beings. To be human, therefore, is to be in relation.

In creation, God allowed us to have the freedom to say yes or no to the divine vision. And here the plot thickens! We humans proved to be far more interested in our own visions than in God's. We abuse our freedom, set ourselves against God and one another. We create systems that benefit only the most privileged among us. Contrary to

23

the very God-given structure of life, namely, its relational character, we allow our selfish actions to take control. We become estranged from nature, ourselves, each other, and God. The divine image given in creation becomes distorted and defaced, and God's dream and intention of *shalom* meets its deepest resistance in the human being.

But God's love goes on reaching and seeking. God calls a people into being—a people to witness to this vision. Abraham was called to go out into a new land to establish a new people who would express the Creator's purpose. Isaac, Jacob, and Joseph—descendants of Abraham—were called in later generations to express God's divine intention. But, after Joseph's death, there came to power those who "did not know Joseph" and the people of God were enslaved in Egypt. Then, God called Moses to liberate the people from oppression and developed them into a new covenant people for a new land. The covenant call to God's people was not a call to special rights but to special responsibilities. The people of God were responsible to be a "light to the nations" (Isa. 49:6). As a covenant people, they were challenged to live a distinctively different life than the other nations of the world. Therefore, the law, expressing the content of the covenant, was given. But, again, God's action and vision were thwarted, for the people turned to disobedience and idolatry. God continued to raise up prophets to keep alive a faithful remnant who would not lose sight of the Creator's vision. But the people "stoned the messengers and the prophets."

Still God did not give up. The depth of human sin required a correspondingly deep and profound remedy. So God acted again, entering our human condition, becoming incarnate in Jesus of Nazareth. *Shalom* was born at Bethlehem. As Paul put it, "Jesus Christ is our peace." He is our liberator—the light of the world. Through Jesus the good news of the kingdom was announced. Through Jesus, the Word became flesh and dwelt among us. But in our sin and rebellion, we nailed the ultimate expression of God's love to a rugged cross. However, in the act of dying upon the cross, Jesus manifested the awesome love of God delivering us from bondage to the principalities and powers. And in the resurrection, God proved that it is *love*, and not any worldly power or force, that makes the world go around. God proved that love is the first principle of the universe. So the good news of God's deliverance was actualized in the dawn of the new age in Jesus of Nazareth in his victory of life over death, love over hate, reconciliation over alienation.

24

The message of the kingdom in the preaching of Jesus was the good news that God's sovereign reign was beginning. In the advent and ministry of Jesus Christ this decisive reign of God had its dawning. The urgency of entering the new age pulsates in the preaching of Jesus—"The time is fulfilled and the kingdom of God is at hand" (Mark 1:15). Jesus' invitation is to enter God's kingdom with the consequence that a radical new relationship with God is established. To enter the kingdom of God requires that a person repent of his or her citizenship in the old age and turn toward the new. While the consummation of the new age is to come, the power of the new age is already operative in the ministry of Jesus. The blind see, the deaf hear, the lame walk, and the poor hear the gospel. Thus, Jesus' invitation to the kingdom is an invitation to a new life characterized by repentance, faith, and loving obedience. Those who enter the kingdom are those who have turned from the old world of bondage to principalities and powers and have placed their trust in God. As members of God's kingdom they are to live for God and others.

Those who hear the call and enter the kingdom are given the task of sharing God's love with one another and with the world. Thus, God calls into being a new people—a new community responsible to live with their Creator and with one another in a fellowship of covenant love and loyalty. This new community is a special creation by virtue of God's call. It is a community which owes its existence, its solidarity, and its corporate distinctness from other communities to one thing only—the call of God. Thus the church is God's people, God's *ekklesia*, called out of the world, called into the fellowship of Christ and sent back into the world to preach, teach, suffer, serve, and heal. Even as God did not call Abraham just to be Abraham, or the twelve disciples just to be the twelve disciples, but to become the people of God, so the church is not called to privilege but to special responsibility.

This community of faith becomes the new Israel—the church—and its creation by God has the whole world and all the people as its backdrop. God's church is a new messianic community in which Jew and Gentile are together as fellow citizens, branches of one olive tree, and brothers and sisters in one family. The spirit of the risen Christ dwells within them and they find themselves participating in a new creation, a new order of redeemed relationships set in the midst of the old order of broken relationships. Thus, Jesus' promise to build the church becomes a historical reality and the church takes root in the soil of the Mediterranean world.

Through the gift of the Holy Spirit at Pentecost (Acts 2), the church was empowered to witness to God's saving activity. At Pentecost, a missionary church was formed. The Holy Spirit empowered that community with the gifts necessary to participate in God's mission in the world. The new messianic community began to spread the Christian story throughout the world. They lived and moved in the conviction that the risen Christ was available to everyone and at every geographical point.

The risen Christ was and is present in the world. Thus, being filled with the Holy Spirit, the church went forth to spread the gospel and to develop congregations all over their world. Each congregation became a missionary congregation. Out of gratitude for God's grace and compassion for the lost, and obedience to Jesus' command, those early Christians went forth preaching the gospel of the kingdom, making disciples and planting churches. The thrust of their message was reconciliation to God—the point of the whole drama of salvation both for individuals and for all creation. They were captivated by God's vision of *shalom*. Thus they issued the call to leave behind the kingdom of sin, corruption, and evil for the kingdom of God, for life, righteousness, peace, and justice.

Now it is the widespread loss of confidence in the truth, the power and relevance of this gospel of the kingdom which impedes church development. For not only is the gospel of the kingdom the saving power of God, it is also that which energizes the church with expectancy and hope. Without the message of the gospel of the kingdom, life cannot be lived in joy, expectancy, and hope. And without these the church gives an uncertain sound and its members do not gird themselves for battle. They grow weary in well-doing. They suffer "compassion fatigue." They become quite content with a "four-walls mentality." The revitalization of existing congregations and the development of new ones is not their priority. Therefore, one of the most incessant tasks of our day is to kindle the true hope of the gospel of the kingdom, the lack of which causes our people to pursue the will-of-the-wisps of secular illusion whose fruit is ashes and whose end is despair.

RECOMMENDATIONS FOR CONGREGATIONAL DEVELOPMENT/REDEVELOPMENT

Now that we have explored both the rationale and roots of our theological task, what recommendations can we garner to guide us

26

in the revitalization of existing congregations and the development of new ones?

1. According to the gospel story, congregational development comes as a result of God's activity and has its origin in the very nature of the Trinity. The Bible leaves no doubt that the Creator is a living, loving, envisioning, willing, acting spirit—a personal God (Exod. 3:14; Eph. 1:1-11). From the Creation and Fall and throughout history, God has always been in search of the lost. Moreover, God seeks us down the corridors of time. God is revealed throughout history. The living God has meaning in the context of history and in dialogue with persons. Thus, the living God of the scriptures is not outside time and space, a kind of motionless, abstract essence. The living God is one whose heart feels and longs and loves; one whose voice speaks; one who intervenes, acts, seeks, sends, and suffers. This redeeming God comes into the broken order of our lives to dwell with us in person-to-person relationships. The living God is a missionary God.

The gospel story highlights the initiative of God. It teaches us that we never take God by surprise. God is always "in the beginning"—making the first move. We cannot predate the initiative of God. God seeks us long before our seeking begins. This initiatory activity of God is seen in our doctrine of the Trinity. We have a vision of *God as Father* through God's sending activity to all humankind and God's perpetual working in creation. *God as Son* is the climactic expression of God's sending and seeking love. God comes to us in the incarnation. Now, through Jesus Christ, a relationship with God is made available to all persons. It is through Christ that we and our world are reconciled to God. Jesus gives final substance to the word *love*. Since God's love has such a concrete, historical reference, it is not a matter of mythical or simply ethical ideals. It is, rather, substantial love available to all. Jesus Christ is the exponent of God's love in action (Acts 15), and the exemplar who by deeds of compassion reveals love again and again. Christ loves not only the old, the lonely, the poor, the weak, and the despised; that love even reaches out to rich young rulers. *God as Holy Spirit* empowers and sends the church forth to love others for no other reason than the fact that they are human beings, and not because they are "our kind of people," or agreeable, or attractive, or lovable.

Love is the essential characteristic of the nature of God (1 John 4:8-16). All Christian love is a derivative of God's love. The heart of our theology is the fact that the living God is manifested as love. The realization that we are supported, surrounded, and sought by a final reality which we call love is the most amazing, incomprehensible, and marvelous fact of human existence. Upon this reality congregational development will either rise or fall, because here we stand at the center of everything. Our attempt to understand congregational development in theological perspective will be an elaboration of this wonderful reality.

2. The development of congregations is God's idea and not merely a human achievement. As we have seen, the Bible is concerned with creating a people of God. Peter summarized a quotation from Exodus 19:5-6 when he declared, "You are a chosen group, a royal priesthood, a holy nation, God's own people, that you may declare the wonderful deeds of him who called you out of darkness into his marvelous light" (2 Pet. 2:9). This call relates to God's personal and relational nature.

The fact that God's seeking love reaches out to us through the history of patriarchs and prophets, and ultimately through the person of Jesus Christ, is ample proof that God speaks to persons through persons. Our love for persons follows from our love for God. This affirms the personal and relational nature of God and says that it is impossible for us to exist as Christians apart from this world of the personal and relational. It also implies that God never enters into a personal relationship with an individual apart from other persons.

Therefore, it is the will of God that the people of God should be drawn together in congregational support. The gospel story knows little about a private religion unrelated to the larger body of believers, the congregation. For this reason the Christian call is always at least a two-fold call: a call to respond to God, and a call to respond to one another. For instance, Paul uses the terms *in Christ* or *in the Lord* approximately two hundred times. Though at times he means a mystical union with Christ seen in terms of personal relationship (Gal. 3:27), most of the time he means being a part of the fellowship of believers in Christ, or the community of faith. When he speaks of the church as a body with Christ as the head, he uses the concept of an organism featuring a shared life, a koinonia bound together.

To be Christian, therefore, is more than an individual experience; it is a social experience. One might become a Christian by an individual response but even in that process one is born into a family—a fellowship. Moreover, this fellowship offers more than mere togetherness; it is a sharing in the Body of Christ. As far as I

28

can tell, the New Testament knows nothing of a "go it alone" religion. Bonhoeffer stated this truth forthrightly:

> Into the community you were called, the call was not meant for you alone; in the community of the called you bear your cross, you struggle, you pray. You are not alone. Even in death and on the Last Day you will be only one member of the great congregation of Jesus Christ. If you scorn the fellowship of the brethren, you reject the call of Jesus Christ, and thus your solitude can only be hurtful to you.[2]

One of the major misconceptions of Christianity in North America is that it is individualistic rather than corporate. This is due partly to a limitation in our language and the individualistic mindset of the Anglo-Saxon. Unfortunately, standard English does not provide a clear differentiation between second person singular and plural. Given the Anglo mindset, we tend to read the New Testament as though it were all addressed to individuals. It is clear, however, in the Greek that the word *you* is in the plural and refers to the congregation as a whole. But our individualism produces distortions which cause us to miss this point and view the church primarily as a means to help the individual "get saved."[3] Therefore, we tend to build up *individuals* in the faith whereas the New Testament uses that phraseology primarily to talk about building up *congregations* in the faith. Theologically, it is God's intention to build community and not just individual piety. God's intent is for us to be together in community and to learn how to live in love, justice, and peace.

3. Since congregational development is God's idea and not the institutional church's invention, it follows that congregational development is not merely an ecclesiological phenomenon but a theological one. God has not afforded the church the luxury of debating whether or not congregational development is necessary, as if it were the church's idea. Once we realize that congregational development is God's idea—an expression of God's unswerving purpose—then our choice is either to be obedient or disobedient. If we are obedient, congregational development will become our priority and the church will pray and work toward that end.

It is necessary to see God as both the originator and initiator of congregational development in order to offset the impression that congregational development is merely a human achievement. This is precisely the impression given when the church allows itself to slip into the outlook of secular culture and supposes that the key to congregational development is technological efficiency, and that congregational development happens automatically if we will only follow the instructions given in "do-it-yourself" manuals. The story in Acts of the spread of the gospel and the growth of congregations is not so much a "how-to-do-it manual." Precious little emphasis is given to "one-two-three step" methods. Massive emphasis is given to the invigorating power of the Holy Spirit, the spread of the gospel, and the faith that developed in response to the hearing of the Word of God. The growth of congregations in Acts is not a tribute to human ingenuity and enterprise, but a witness to the prevailing power of the Holy Spirit working through the church. The gospel story corrects our all-too-prevalent tendency to make human activity the center of everything, as if all we need is to discover new techniques. Let us remember that methods are important as means, but demonic as ends, and that methods must grow out of the gospel story which shapes and judges our methods.

4. Basic to the development of new congregations and the revitalization of existing ones, and right at the heart of the church's vocation in the world, is the sense of mission inherent in the proclamation of the kingdom of God. Quite simply, the kingdom means God's rule as it relates to persons, peoples, societies, and history. Under God's redeeming Lordship the whole creation will finally be transformed in terms of God's vision of *shalom.*

Jesus Christ saw the church in the light of this kingdom orientation and established it as a vital part of God's mission to bring in a new order of things. This new order dawned in the ministry and message of Jesus and will be completed by him. It is an order of life wherein all relationships will be put right, not only between God and people but also among people, nations, sexes, generations, and races, and even between people and their ecological environment. It is in this sense that the kingdom is the fulfillment of God's vision of *shalom,* and it is to this vision the apostles testified when they spoke of looking forward to a new heaven and a new earth where justice dwells (2 Pet. 3:13). If the eschatological pull of this dynamic kingdom ceases to be our major incentive in congregational development, then we can rest assured that we have "missed the mark."

The congregations we develop must be kingdom-oriented. The gospel leaves no doubt but that God intends the church to be a new society which models the kingdom. Thus the kingdom of God must

30

be at the center of the church's life, even as it was at the heart of the preaching and teaching of Jesus. Only as local churches are reflections of the universal church and its relation to the kingdom can they be faithful to the biblical pattern. It is their kingdom orientation which gives local churches eschatological dimensions and makes them more than the pragmatic achievements of scientific principles. It is their relation to the kingdom which pushes local churches beyond their individualistic and materialistic tendencies, helping them see that being the church is more than enlisting a lot of people and erecting extravagant buildings to put them in.[4] It is the local church's kingdom orientation that enables it to become a training ground for lay missionary work rather than a maintenance operation. It is the kingdom orientation which draws the local church outside itself and points it toward a hurting world. To be kingdom-oriented means that the local church is essentially evangelistic and missionary, or it is not the church.

All of us believe the development of local churches comes as a result of our faithful response to the call of the kingdom of God. In our minds, local churches and the kingdom are closely related. But, we must never forget, it is the kingdom that determines the nature of local churches. This order must never be reversed. The kingdom is first; churches are second. The primary call is to the kingdom. This difficult distinction must be maintained lest we forget that our local churches are always something less than the kingdom, while at the same time they are a vital and necessary part.[5]

If this order is prayerfully maintained, we will refuse the temptation to compromise the substance of the gospel in order to attain success. We all know that our passion for numerical success and power often tempts us to offer "cheap grace." But the kingdom demands that we balance success with substance. The prevailing mood of our success-oriented society is that we must dress up the gospel and the church to make them palatable. Thus, the substance of the gospel is tailored to fit the wants of sophisticated consumers who are looking for a religion with no suffering, no serving, no cross. This pseudo-gospel is marketed in such a way as to be sellable—without making significant ethical demands upon the buyer.[6]

This temptation to accommodate to prevailing cultural moods is pervasive to the degree that it could impact our programs of congregational development. It could cause us to sidestep kingdom standards. This can be seen in the fact that, for some, the principles for planting and revitalizing congregations are more determined by sociological and scientific data than by the gospel. Witness how we tend to do ministry where we are reasonably sure of numerical success. This strong emphasis upon concentrating on target populations where success is guaranteed could cause us to neglect the city with its economic fickleness, changing neighborhoods, and racial complexity. It could cause us to always take the easy way.[7]

But, if the kingdom order is maintained, we will be reminded that as kingdom people we are called to a radical new allegiance, new citizenship, and new demands, and that the biblical emphasis is not so much on how easy but how costly it is to be kingdom people. If the proper order is maintained, our passion for numerical success and power will be checked by kingdom standards which hold up the loving, serving, suffering Christ as our model. If the proper order is maintained, our temptation for self-preservation as an institution will be offset by the kingdom call to lay down our lives in suffering service, even as Jesus gave himself in serving the poor and wretched of the earth. His obedience in mission is the kingdom standard for kingdom people.

Since Jesus' proclamation of the gospel to the poor is a concrete sign of the kingdom of God, it also becomes a powerful criterion by which we judge the validity of our congregational development. It will mean that mission analysis always gains ascendance over demographic analysis and that we concentrate larger and larger amounts of human and material resources in our cities, among the poor of the earth, and with struggling ethnic minorities.

The conclusion of all this could be stated as follows: Sociological studies, pragmatism, and keen management skills are all necessary resources for the development of congregations and revitalization of existing ones. But all these resources must be informed and critiqued by the gospel and seen as only a part of the larger theological context. We dare not elevate sociological data and commercial marketing techniques beyond our mandate to be faithful to the theological task. No success orientation can be allowed to supplant our orientation as kingdom people. I am confident that this insistence upon theological integrity and clarity will not impede but, rather, enhance the overall growth of the church. That first century church certainly grew precisely *because* it had its priorities straight.

---

1. For a more complete statement see George E. Morris, *The Mystery and Meaning of Christian Conversion* (Nashville, Tennessee: Discipleship Resources, 1981).

2. Dietrich Bonhoeffer, *Life Together,* translated and with an introduction by John W. Doberstein (New York: Harper and Brothers, 1954), pp. 97-99.

3. Michael Griffiths, *The Church and World Mission* (Grand Rapids, Michigan: Zondervan, 1980), p. 40. See also George E. Morris, *The Mystery and Meaning of Christian Conversion,* pp. 149-156.

4. Justice C. Anderson, "The Nature of Churches," *The Birth of Churches,* ed. Talmadge R. Amberson (Nashville, Tennessee: Broadman Press, 1979), pp. 50-54.

5. Ralph H. Elliott, *Church Growth That Counts* (Valley Forge, PA: Judson Press, 1982), pp. 69-72.

6. Ibid., p. 91.

7. Ibid., p. 74.

Chapter 4

The Vital Congregation:
Socio-Cultural Factors

Luther E. Smith, Jr.

God seeks a servant people. This affirmation comes from the biblical account of God's interaction with humanity. We are called to commit ourselves to manifesting God's will and power and to revealing that the fullness of life is experienced in faithfulness to our Creator and Redeemer. Such a people are abundantly alive and enlivening and constitute the vital congregation.

Religious beliefs, fellowship, ritual, and education are crucial to the vitality of the congregation. These essentials nurture persons in the precepts and activity of faith. Members of the congregation, however, are also shaped by the socio-cultural realities of their lives. These realities are not abandoned when they participate in the church. Into the church's life members bring their poverty, wealth, racial identity, ethnic consciousness, social influence, sense of oppression, cultural aspirations, and political convictions. These are factors which not only shape individuals, but shape local churches and denominations as well.

H. Richard Niebuhr, in his classic *The Social Sources of Denominationalism*, documents how socio-cultural factors have been the bases for separation, prejudice, and stratification which threaten the realization of the kingdom of God. Too often when the church has engaged these factors, it has retreated from the gospel's demands for love and unity. But such factors are not only cause for retreat, they are opportunities for servanthood. Socio-cultural realities call forth the profoundest understandings and applications of our faith. These realities are the crucible for faith. And to those servants who accept this challenge, God promises vitality.

THE WORLD IS OUR PARISH

The world is God's holy creation. God continues to express love and renewing power in and through the created order. The church's mission, therefore, is not to rescue people from the world (God's dwelling place), but to be an instrument which reconciles the world to God. This reconciliation is not the reuniting of a "spoiled" creation with the Creator, for God has never been separated from creation. This reconciliation occurs when the world submits to the rule of God. It is a rule characterized by justice, freedom, and healing. Jesus began his ministry with such an understanding. In the synagogue he read from the Book of Isaiah:

"The Spirit of the Lord is upon me, because he has anointed me to preach good news to the poor. He has sent me to proclaim release to the captives and recovering of sight to the blind, to set at liberty those who are oppressed, to proclaim the acceptable year of the Lord." And he closed the book, and gave it back to the attendant, and sat down; and the eyes of all in the synagogue were fixed on him. And he began to say to them, "Today this scripture has been fulfilled in your hearing" (Luke 4:18-21).

The church as the Body of Christ has the mission to continue this holy activity. The world is the context for it.

Evangelism is witnessing to the world so that it recognizes its brokenness and participates in the reconciling process. The vital congregation's witness to socio-cultural issues is made without the requirement that its evangelistic efforts result in the increase of its membership. Evangelism is not contingent upon membership growth.

Much of a church's witness to world realities is to systems, conditions, and public policy where membership is not at issue. Reconciling activities that challenge apartheid in South Africa or the abuse of human rights in El Salvador are not likely to cause South Africans or Salvadorans to request church membership. Labors to halt the nuclear arms race or to end world hunger will not fill church rolls. These activities are the church's selfless involvement in the world. They are done for the glory of God.

Evangelism within a church's local community should have the same selfless motivation. Fellowship with and caring for one's neighbors are important because they express the reconciling love of God. Love is unconditional. Neither membership needs, nor budget deficits, nor denominational pressures are proper motivations for loving.

In urban areas across the nation many predominantly white congregations are in the midst of predominantly black communities. At one time the community reflected the racial composition of the congregations. But a variety of forces (such as desegregation policies, racial prejudice, the availability of better housing, the loss of commercial establishments, or a city's urban strategy) may have caused whites to leave and blacks to become residents. Most of the white churches that stayed in their community have experienced anxiety, confusion, and frustration in developing relationships with their black neighbors. Bridging the separation of blacks and whites is not easily done. And yet many of these churches have concluded that it is necessary to initiate evangelistic efforts in behalf of their black residents. Why? Motivation must be rooted in love. Black residents can sense when they are a means to an end, when they are sought to help a church survive, or appease guilt, or fill pews.

The world is not just a place from which a congregation recruits prospective members to the reconciling ground of the church. Reconciliation must occur in the world, at the places where people live, work, and play. If black residents already belong to a church, or if they are not attracted to a white church, are they to be ignored? Each year students in my classes are required to interview pastors and discern how the church relates to its community. When pastors are asked why their church is not more involved in the community, the vast majority respond: "The residents are not likely to join this particular church." This attitude prevents congregations from being reconciled to their brothers and sisters in the community. A church's involvement with its neighbors enables members and residents to relate to each other in sensitive and caring ways. Christian fellowship becomes possible, manifesting God's love and reconciling power. And the vitality of restored relationships is experienced by the congregation and community. The world is our parish, and our parish is the context for reconciliation.

Communities contain not only complex socio-cultural problems but also socio-cultural resources. How often the kingdom of God is experienced by the poor (Lk. 6:20), their utter dependency upon God revealing the Redeemer's power in ways that inspire faith. In listening to their stories one can hear how God provides in the midst of hunger and homelessness. Along with their cries of agony one can hear joy and hope in response to despairing conditions.

Jean Vanier, the founder of l'Arche (a ministry of living with and helping the mentally handicapped), tells of going to visit a house where the severely handicapped reside. None of the persons could talk, and several could not walk. Vanier's whole way of communicat-

36

ing and expecting had to change in order for him to be in relationship with them. He testifies that this change brought rest to his tiredness and enabled him to "recognize the presence of God." Vanier concludes, "The poorest people have an extraordinary power to heal the wounds in our hearts. If we welcome them, they nourish us."[1]

God is in the midst of the poor, the handicapped, the refugees, the prisoners, the strangers, and the oppressed. Ministry to sociocultural realities does not just drain church resources, it clarifies vision and revitalizes commitment. In community God awaits us and meets our needs. The world is our parish, and our parish is the context for revitalization.

THE INCLUSIVE CHURCH

The world looks at the church's fellowship to discern the meaning of the reconciling word it professes. Reconciliation that is manifest within the church authenticates its role as an agent of reconciliation—not just to prove something to society, but because God desires a reconciled church. The church's ability to witness to sociocultural differences is a primary sign of vitality.

The birth of the church on the day of Pentecost began with just such a witness. The apostles were "filled with the Holy Spirit and began to speak in other tongues, as the Spirit gave them utterance" (Acts 2:4). And a multitude comprised of Parthians, Medes, Elamites; residents of Mesopotamia, Judea, Cappadocia, Pontus, Asia, Phrygia, Pamphylia, Egypt, parts of Libya belonging to Cyrene; visitors from Rome, Crete, and Arabia proclaimed, "We hear them telling in our own tongues the mighty works of God" (Acts 2:5-13). The Holy Spirit empowers God's servants in the midst of diversity to address the needs of a diverse world. This witness challenges a postulate of the church growth movement which states: "Disciples are more readily made by people within their own homogeneous unit, and congregations develop into healthy communities when they concentrate on only one kind of people."[2]

The tendency for persons to join churches because of the membership's similarity with their socio-economic status is well documented.[3] Being with "our kind of people" is often portrayed as the "natural" grouping which goes on within any society. The grouping is based on tradition, lifestyle, and values which members hold in common. Challenges to such groups are considered idealistic critiques which only offer "artificial" solutions for heterogeneity. This notion of natural and artificial is specious reasoning. Homogeneity is not a benign selection process. Blacks and whites have been separated by law. The lending practices of financial institutions, the selling practices of real estate firms, and the policies of insurance companies have conspired to create racially and economically segregated neighborhoods. Urban development and business location decisions have maintained patterns of racial and economic a-partheid. Much of what is described as natural homogeneity is founded upon the evils of discrimination, prejudice, hatred, and avarice. Even if these evils are accepted as a social norm of behavior, and therefore fitting the definition of "natural," they cannot be accepted as natural in the kingdom of God. All are family before God. And reconciliation is natural, even when it may appear extreme, as in the welcoming of a prodigal child.

Homogeneity is also sought by requiring potential group members to abandon those values and cultural qualities which are different from the group's. Being assimilated into a group means being stripped of essential characteristics which have given one identity. Reconciliation is not assimilation. Reconciliation affirms one's history and identity. It recognizes the richness of diverse perspectives. What is first perceived by a congregation as odd may serve to revitalize its fellowship and worship. The congregation's ability to "sing unto the Lord a new song" (Psalm 96) may come from persons who bring new insights and traditions into its life.

The vitality of reconciliation does not simply occur when diverse people are physically close to one another. In the cafeterias of many integrated high schools I have seen tables with only white students and tables with only black students. The educational system put them within the same building but did not integrate their unstructured socializing. Reconciliation goes beyond being physically present with one another. It is a quality of welcome, trust, respect, and caring to the extent that understanding and love characterize the fellowship.

Prospective church members look for congregations where warmth and concern prevail. In Roger A. Johnson's study of congregations, persons were asked to rank factors "which contributed to their decision to join their present church." The result was:

"The friendliness of members" received the highest response (47%). When asked to rate what factors would influence their choice of a new congregation, respondents ranked "the fellowship of members with each other" highest.[4]

Edward A. Rauff's *Why People Join the Church* explores the various reasons people decide upon church membership. He discusses personal crises, the influence of Christians, family relationships, responses to evangelism, terminating rebellion, and reactions to guilt, fear, and emptiness. In a section entitled "The Search for Community" he writes:

> Of the many factors that lead unchurched people to church membership, fellowship is one that seems most ripe for implementing. We can't manufacture crises in people's lives, nor can we easily manipulate family pressures to nudge someone closer to the church doors. But there may be ways to raise the consciousness of church members to empathize with the stranger and observe some rules of church sociability.[5]

Sensitivity to the desire for a warm fellowship helps to create conditions for reconciliation. But more than friendliness is needed. Reconciliation requires intimacy. Jesus' way of establishing relationships is illustrative. He was not just friendly with the Samaritan woman at the well. He knew her to the extent that she "went her way into the city, and said to the people, 'Come, see a man who told me all that I ever did' " (John 4:28-29).

Yet there are strong socio-cultural pressures to maintain racial and ethnic boundaries which prevent intimacy between different groups. In 1944 Gunnar Myrdal in his major work, *An American Dilemma*, ranked types of discrimination which whites maintained against blacks. Least objectionable, to whites, were the efforts blacks made to earn a living or receive aid from social welfare programs. Objection was more intense for blacks who sought to end discrimiation in law courts, political disfranchisement, and segregated public facilities. Whites most objected to interracial socializing, fraternization, and marriage.[6] Lest one think this is an outdated conclusion, a study conducted from 1972 to 1976 revealed that nearly 50 percent of churched Protestants surveyed believed there should be laws against blacks and whites marrying.[7]

Milton M. Gordon's *Assimilation in American Life* analyzes the fear of intimacy in discussing the concept of structural separation. Structural separation is defined as "a situation in which primary group contacts between members of various ethnic groups are held to a minimum, even though secondary contacts on the job, on the civic scene, and in other areas of impersonal contact may abound."[8] The maintenance of structural separation characterizes the American experience. Yet Gordon warns, "It may be plausibly argued that just as intimate primary group relations tend to reduce prejudice, a lack of such contacts tends to promote ethnically hostile attitudes."[9]

Structural separation is even part of church mission. I am aware of a church that conducts an extensive program of feeding and sheltering homeless people. The homeless are the poorest of the poor. This is evident in their appearance. Parishioners were proud of their outreach. And all was well until some of the homeless began to attend Sunday morning worship and then would come to the coffee fellowship hour after worship. Having the poor on one side of the counter receiving sandwiches was one thing, but to worship and fellowship as equals was quite disturbing to many members. Even more troubling was the prospect that the homeless might decide to visit members at their homes.

Reconciliation without intimacy is deficient, coming short of the kingdom of God. Socio-cultural concerns are not to be kept at the level of issues. Reconciliation is between people and is not just attention given to the conditions of people. Poverty, hunger, and injustice exist within the lives of persons who are to be known and related to intimately. Howard Thurman, cofounder of one of the first interracial and intercultural churches in America, asserts the importance of knowing another person's "fact." A person's fact includes more than one's condition; it is also his or her potential. He writes:

> Intrinsic interest must be informed, and constantly. There is no substitute for hard understanding of more and more and more of another's fact. This serves as a corrective against doing violence to those for whom we have a sense of caring because of great gaps in our knowledge of their fact. This is generally the weakness in so much lateral good will in the world. It is uninformed, ignorant, sincere good will. . . . I think that this is why it is impossible to have intrinsic interest in people with whom we are out of living or vicarious contact.[10]

Statistics about the church's community can provide significant information on the people and the trends of an area. Mission committees, however, need to place more emphasis on getting to know their neighbors through conversation and fellowship rather than gathering census data about them. Surveys, community studies, and computer printouts may be shields against intimacy rather than tools for understanding.

Intimacy means exposure of one's total self. Revealed are not only one's abilities, but weaknesses; not only one's faith, but doubt; not only one's resources, but the inadequacy of those resources; not only one's concern, but indifference; not only one's gifts, but needs. Stripped of pretense, one's own poverty becomes real. Socio-cultural factors cease to determine relations by a superior-inferior dynamic. It is then that one is fully available to another, and to God. In this poverty comes vitality. Blessed is our poverty, for through it we come to know the kingdom of God (Luke 6:20).

POTENT WORSHIP

The vital congregation is nurtured by vital worship. Worship is central to the church's life. Brought before God are one's poverty, job, and seeking. Persons hunger and thirst for meaning in their lives and the power to fulfill the demands of their days.

Vital worship addresses socio-cultural realities. "The earth and the fullness thereof" are defined as God's. Faithful stewardship of this earth is sought through prayer, hearing the Word proclaimed, and renewal of commitment. World concerns, therefore, are an integral part of the worship experience.

Some members of the congregation feel estranged from socio-cultural realities. The world is a confusing, evil place from which they seek asylum in worship. Others are at home in the world, yet fail to practice their faith in the midst of it. Religious life and social life are distinct realities which often have no intercourse. There are members who are involved daily in determining the outcome of socio-cultural realities, yet they become weary in well-doing. They need their Christian identity affirmed in the midst of what seems like only humanism. Worship is the opportunity to meet these hungers of the spirit. Preaching rooted in the scriptures does not promote a particular social, economic, or political philosophy, but defines socio-cultural matters as sacred concerns. The world is our parish when the vitality of God is known to extend beyond the sanctuary to life itself.

Vitality for worship resides in the traditions of people outside a local congregation. I am dismayed to hear white churches consider-

41

ing the black spirituals only as an evangelistic tool to recruit black members. The spirituals communicate a deep religious understanding which crosses cultural boundaries. They inspire, and therefore should be appreciated on their own merit as songs of faith.

Asians and Hispanics reveal rich understandings of God's activity in their histories and cultures. Their preaching, singing, praying, and liturgy can expand a congregation's vision of celebrating being the people of God. This is not an appeal for techniques that spice up a service. Worship is not the occasion for gimmicks that entertain. Neither is it an appeal for churches to abandon long-held traditions. Tradition is to be celebrated, for it provides inspiration and continuity. What is needed, however, is the realization that socio-cultural differences can contribute to the vitality of worship. The inclusive church is open to persons from different churches and to religious expressions conceived in various cultural contexts.

Worship can be an experience of intimacy with persons from varied socio-cultural backgrounds. Songs, liturgy, preaching, and prayer can affirm the identity of kinship and equality before God. Henri Nouwen writes how prayer works the miracle of intimacy:

It [prayer] does not mean worrying together, but becoming present for each other in a very real way. . . . What we then ask from each other is not, first of all, to solve a problem or to give a hand, but to affirm each other in the many different ways we experience life. When this takes place, community starts to form and becomes a reality that can be celebrated as an affirmation of the multiformity of being in which we all take part.[11]

The intimacy with others and with God during worship empowers the congregation. The power comes, not out of deeds of reconciliation that earn vitality, but from the grace and mystery of God. It is this power which is necessary to confront the recalcitrant forces that would use socio-cultural factors to promote an ethic of separation. This power overcomes the congregation's resistance to "a new song" in worship. It is the power to be the servant people of God.

The vitality is available to congregations of all sizes and in all places. I have seen churches of twenty-five people more corporately involved in reconciliation than churches of 2500. God seeks a servant people; size and location are not barriers. A church may not have a talented music director, dynamic preacher, or charismatic lay leader who skillfully enacts the vision of reconciliation. But God provides resources for faithful witness.

A congregation's commitment and willingness to sacrifice can determine its ability to triumph over limitations. More money for missions may not be needed, but a redistribution of present finances may be required. Rather than more people, a congregation may need a rededication of present members to reconciliation. Instead of initiating a flood of new social programs, the transformation of Christian education, prayer meetings, and evangelism to address justice concerns may well be in order.

Revitalization comes through struggle. And in the process some things die so that others can be formed. Christian witness requires losing life to find new life in Christ (Luke 9:24). Owen D. Owens' *Growing Churches for a New Age* provides ten case studies of renewed congregations. Reflecting upon the common experiences of these churches he says: "Almost without exception *new life broke into these congregations out of shattering, or dissolving, of what they had been.*"[12] Conflict, misunderstanding, uncertainty, and the reality (not just the threat) of death are involved when a congregation says yes to God. But the congregation also has the promise of God's love which can sustain it through all phases of living, and dying, and living again. And for a people of faith, this is enough.

1. Jean Vanier, *Community and Growth* (New York: Paulist Press, 1979), pp. 117-118.

2. C. Peter Wagner, *Our Kind of People* (Atlanta: John Knox, 1979), p. 4.

3. See H. Paul Chalfant, Robert E. Beckley, and C. Eddie Palmer, *Religion in Contemporary Society* (Sherman Oaks, CA: Alfred Publishing, 1981), pp. 372-387, for a discussion of research correlating socio-cultural status and church affiliation.

4. Roger A. Johnson, *Congregations as Nurturing Communities* (Division for Parish Services, Lutheran Church in America, 1979), p. 35.

5. Edward A. Rauff, *Why People Join the Church* (New York: Pilgrim Press; Washington, D.C.: Glenmary Research, 1979), p. 87.

6. New York: Harper & Brothers, 1944, pp. 60-61.

7. David A. Roozen, *The Churched and the Unchurched in America* (Washington, D.C.: Glenmary Research Center, 1978), p. 44.

8. Milton M. Gordon, *Assimilation in American Life* (New York: Oxford University, 1964), p. 235.

9. Ibid., pp. 235-236.

10. Howard Thurman, *Mysticism and the Experience of Love* (Wallingford, PA: Pendle Hill, 1961), p. 15.

11. Henri Nouwen, *Creative Ministry* (Garden City, NY: Image, 1978), p. 97.

12. Owen D. Owens, *Growing Churches for a New Age* (Valley Forge, PA: Judson, 1981), p. 189.

Chapter 5

The Nature and Function of the Parish In a Changing World

Robert L. Wilson

The parish church, like the nuclear family, has been one of society's most durable institutions. It has existed and continues to exist in a wide range of cultures. It has survived in political systems which were friendly and in those which were hostile. Despite substantial differences in the organization of the parent denominations, the local churches have continued to carry on their task. While denominations tend to make frequent alterations in their structures and nomenclature, not much seems to change in the local churches. It is almost as if the parish has a life of its own that enables it to defy, or at least ignore, the changes which the parent denomination may seek to impose on it.

The parish has been the building block out of which denominations are constructed. It is the local churches which provide both the leaders and the funds that make denominational structures possible. Both denominational and ecumenical organizations rest upon the base of the local church.

FOUR BASIC FUNCTIONS

The parish provides the setting where four basic functions are performed. The first is *proclamation.* It is here that the gospel is preached and the sacraments administered. The parish is where individuals come in contact with the gospel, where they hear or fail to hear the Christian message. When people give their allegiance to the Christian faith, it is usually in the local parish.

The second service is *nurture and education.* The parish provides ways for persons to learn about the Christian faith. The parish socializes individuals into the Christian way of life and helps them grow in their understanding.

A third function which the parish performs is *support* for its members. Many of life's most significant events are interpreted and given meaning by the parish. These include birth, marriage, and death. The members of the local church share each other's joys and sorrows. The individual is made aware of the transcendent and helped to realize that there is an eternity beyond time.

Fourth, the local parish carries out the *mission* of the church. Christianity is a missionary religion which continually seeks to share its faith with those who are outside the church. It does this through witnessing and carrying out a variety of programs in the local community. It supports specialized agencies that witness and serve in distant places on behalf of the congregation. These are an extension of the mission of the congregation.

The parish continues to perform these functions. Changes in the society continue to alter the context in which the parish exists. In some ways the work of the parish is made easier; in other ways the task has been made more difficult. Nevertheless, the basic functions remain and will continue to be performed by the local church.

Let us examine several trends and their impact on the local parish. Some of these trends are in the larger society; others are within the churches themselves. The effect of some on the parish is positive, while the impact of others is negative.

INCREASING SECULARISM

Not too long ago, factors in the larger society tended to affirm the Christian faith. The local church occupied a larger share of people's time than is the case today. It certainly had less competition than it has now.

Consider the role of the parish church in small town and rural America a couple of generations ago. It not only provided for the spiritual needs of its members, it was the recreational center of the community. The only activity in town might have been the Wednesday night prayer meeting and the Sunday evening service. The situation is vastly different today. Individuals, particularly those living in urban areas, have a wide variety of choices as to how they will use their time. The automobile has given them mobility while the television has provided the option of being entertained without leaving home.

The church faces increasing competition for people's time and attention. They do not necessarily gravitate toward the church to have their social needs met and to find recreation. Thus the church must attract people for primarily religious reasons, not simply wait

45

for them to show up and then see that they are exposed to the faith.

Furthermore, our secular society is becoming increasingly hostile toward organized religion. Many examples could be cited, such as conflict over prayer in the public schools, trouble about the placing of crèches on public property at Christmas, and opposition to the use of religious songs and symbols at Christmas.

A recent issue of *The Christian Century* (May 25, 1983) carried an account of a suit being brought by sixteen persons, including some Protestant clergy and the American Civil Liberties Union, against the President of the United States because he had proclaimed 1983 the "Year of the Bible." Now I don't really think that such a proclamation makes a great deal of difference in the way the Bible will be read and believed. What is significant is the increasing hostility toward the church, of which this incident is simply one example.

America is a pluralistic society. We can expect more antagonism among religious groups and more opposition from nonreligious people. Secularism is a world view, a way of looking at people and society, a system of values. It is a faith which is challenged by the Christian faith. It is not going to roll over and play dead; it will strike out against the embodiment of the Christian faith; i.e., the organized church. This is going to continue and probably intensify. We had better be prepared to deal with it.

CHANGING PATTERNS OF MOBILITY

Moving has long been a part of American life. The adventurous persons early moved West. In recent years we have seen trends such as migration from rural to urban areas, blacks moving from the South to the North and the West, people and industry migrating from the North to the Sunbelt, and continuation of the long-term East-to-West movement. There are two aspects of the current mobility which have had an influence on the functioning of the parish.

First, the high degree of mobility in America has resulted in many persons living far from members of their extended families. Large numbers of persons in nuclear families do not have parents, grandparents, aunts, uncles, or cousins residing in the same community. Such relatives may be hundreds of miles away. This is very different from earlier periods when relatives lived in close proximity. The members were available to support each other. They could share both joys and sorrows and provide help in times of stress.

When persons do not have members of their extended families

living in the same community, the supportive role needs to be filled by some group. The local congregation can meet this need. The Sunday school class or the choir can become a kind of extended family for its members. In small membership churches the whole congregation fulfills this function. It is a need that will continue for vast numbers of persons, particularly those living in the major metropolitan centers. No institution is better equipped to perform this function than the local church.

Second, the degree of mobility has slowed substantially. A larger proportion of the population is resisting relocation. There are three major reasons for this trend. One is the high mortgage rate which in 1982 hit 15.4 percent, a figure more than three times that in 1960. A second is the two-career family. A substantial promotion for one partner may actually result in a reduction of the family income if the spouse cannot find an equivalent position in the new location. A third factor is the cost of relocating a home-owning family which was approximately three times greater in 1982 than in 1973.

For the local church the lessened mobility has two implications. First, it will mean less turnover. Persons will remain members longer. There will be greater opportunity for the congregation to develop into the supportive fellowship which is the substitute for the nuclear family. Second, it will be increasingly important for the church to win new residents before they become settled into the habit of being nonchurchgoers. If new residents are not reached, they may be nonparticipants for the longer period of time they can be expected to reside in the community.

While the local church is influenced by factors in the larger society, how the people define their mission and ministry is at least of equal importance in determining how the parish functions. To these internal factors I want to turn.

THE NATURE OF THE PARISH

One of the debates, albeit not a particularly vocal one, has been over the nature of the parish. Throughout much of this century the local church has been perceived as a microcosm of the community. It was to be representative of the various types of persons residing in the community, i.e., to include the different age, racial, and socio-economic groups. It is not surprising that this understanding developed during the 1920s and 1930s when sociological studies of local communities began to produce more sophisticated data on

47

neighborhoods. For the first time it became possible to compare the social characteristics of a congregation with those of its neighborhood. Out of this came the assumption that the local church should be representative of its immediate community.

Much of the interdenominational church planning in the 1940s and 1950s was based on the assumption that a particular new congregation of a cooperating mainline denomination would serve all of the residents of a particular community. Thus, the developing areas were each assigned to a denomination; one area was to have a Presbyterian church, another a Methodist, etc. This system has never really worked as it was intended. Not all denominations cooperated. Furthermore, people tend to go to the type of church they find meaningful, even if it requires driving beyond their immediate neighborhood.

We now realize that a parish is defined in both geographic and social terms. Given the nature of Protestant churches, active participation requires that the individual be present at least once, and frequently several times a week. One cannot live too far from a church and still be an active member. Most people travel less than fifteen or twenty minutes to get to their church. Thus, geographic factors such as distance, barriers, and highway patterns are important.

The parish is also defined in social terms. People tend to join a church which they find meaningful, where they are comfortable with the style of congregational life and with other members. The decision is complex and influenced by a variety of factors. The result is that congregations tend to have some degree of homogeneity as people select churches where the members share their values. This is hardly a new phenomenon nor is it unique to Protestant churches. It is a characteristic of voluntary organizations whether it be the Choral Society, the American Legion, or the Junior League.

The homogeneity of a congregation helps explain certain things which may worry some church leaders. An example is churches of the same denomination which are located near each other and are seen as a wasteful duplication of effort. In reality, each may consist of different types of persons who would be unlikely to attend the other church. Congregational homogeneity also explains why so few local church mergers are successful in retaining a large proportion of the members of both. Congregational differences are greater than is generally realized. Some persons gravitate to other churches for whatever reasons they find more congenial.

The parish shares some of the characteristics of voluntary social organizations. As long as people have the option of attending several different churches, they will select the one that, for whatever reasons, they find best suited to their needs. This is a fact with which church leaders will have to live.

THE FOCUS OF MINISTRY

There has been in the past decade or two a tendency to downgrade the parish as a place of ministry in comparison to other areas of service. Fortunately, this trend seems to be changing. In the early 1970s there were seminary students with the attitude, "If I can't find anything more significant or interesting to do, I'll take an appointment to a local church." Now most seminary students are preparing to enter the parish ministry.

Nevertheless, there is the feeling that the parish minister occupies the bottom rung of the hierarchical ladder. An attitude is abroad in the church, and particularly within The United Methodist Church, that the real ministry, the ministry that is of the greatest significance, is that which is done by the denominational agencies and not by the congregations. Money which is contributed to the denomination for use outside the local church is somehow perceived to be better utilized or more sanctified than that which is used to pay the pastor's salary, purchase Sunday school literature, and to pay the heat and light bills. This of course is nonsense because money given to causes outside the local congregation is ultimately used for exactly the same kinds of things as in the local church, i.e., to pay salaries, maintain facilities, and purchase program materials.

Congregations, like individuals, can become self-centered and ingrown. It is important that Christian people develop a sense of mission and concern for those outside their immediate circle. It is also true that members give to their church at a level which is significantly less than what might be termed sacrificial.

Nevertheless, the present emphasis on the importance of the denominational program has been such that the local ministry and mission are perceived as being of secondary importance. The problem is not how much money is spent but the attitudes which have been developed over the way the funds are used. The result has been that local people have come to see their congregation as of secondary importance.

Fortunately, this is more of a problem for the clergy than for the laity. Ministers may see their professional advancement as dependent on their loyalty to the denomination, a loyalty that is too often determined by how well their congregation supports the denominational program (i.e., pays the annual assessment). In this perception they may be correct. Thus the ministers come to believe that what is being done "out there" is more important than what is being done in the local parish.

This trend has a negative impact on the parish. It contributes to a sense of works righteousness, the feeling that what we do is more important than who we are. The task of the church is first of all to *be* rather than to *do*, and the present trend places an emphasis on doing. It also tends to make the local people, both clergy and laity, feel that the subsidized ministry in some distant place is somehow more important than what is done in the local community. Both are important but neither should take preeminence. A result can be low morale in the parishes. Next, it gives a sense of importance to the denominational bureaucracy that administers the funds that is unhealthy. A bureaucracy can easily move from an orientation of service to the local church to one which has a life of its own with its own goals and programs.

I am not willing to predict the final outcome of this trend. It is, to a considerable degree, the reason for the growing dissatisfaction with boards and agencies. The tension between the parishes and the denominational agencies will probably continue until the local churches again assert their role as the main focus of ministry.

THE IMPACT OF A LONG-TERM DECLINE

The mainline churches have been in a period of decline for approximately fifteen years. During this period both the number of organized congregations and the membership have declined. During the 1970s, the decreases in the number of churches for several denominations were: Episcopal, 2 percent; United Church of Christ, 6 percent; United Methodist, 5 percent; and United Presbyterian USA, 1 percent. The membership decline was even more dramatic: Episcopal, 15 percent; United Church of Christ, 13 percent; United Methodist, 11 percent; and United Presbyterian USA, 22 percent.

If these figures sound a bit gloomy, it is because they are. Denominational leaders tend to put the best possible interpretation on the data because that is what we want them to do. We are told that the downward slide has "bottomed out" and presumably the trend will start upward. Or we are told that while the membership has declined for the seventeenth consecutive year, we can be encouraged because giving has again shown an increase. (Be sure not to compare giving with the rate of inflation because the results might not be quite so encouraging.)

The long-term downward trend may be creating a problem in the attitude it engenders in some of the church people, particularly the clergy. People have become used to being part of a denomination that has been losing members; they have come to accept that fact and consider it the normal state of affairs. I remember a pastor of a congregation which was decreasing in membership in a community where the population was growing. When I asked him why he thought his church had been declining, he replied that this was just part of a nation-wide trend.

Obviously communities vary widely. Some churches will decrease or remain stable despite heroic efforts on the part of the people and pastors. However, the acceptance of a general decline as normal can insure that it will continue.

Since 1969, The United Methodist Church has received 9,889 persons into the ministry as ordained elders and members of annual conferences in full connection. This number represents 45 percent of all of the active elders in the denomination. Almost one-half of all United Methodist clergy have never served in the denomination at a time when the total membership was increasing. Is this fact having an influence on the way pastors perceive their task? Is it having an impact on the way people have come to see the mission and ministry of their church? Is it making a difference in the way persons outside the church perceive us?

A RENEWED SEARCH FOR VALUES

There is an interest in, perhaps even a return to, traditional values. *U.S. News and World Report* carried an article entitled, "The Nation's Real Values—Still Alive." Several scholars were interviewed. One social historian, Leon Botstein, commented, "The nation's network of values has undergone some alterations in recent years—some additions, some deletions—and it lives."[1]

Americans are searching for values that will give meaning and stability to their lives. Despite the apparent transformations in society in recent years, the article states that inertia may be more important in American history than change.

Other recent studies are showing the increasing importance of religious values. The Connecticut Mutual Life Insurance Company examined the values of leaders and the general population. The report stated:

Yet in investigating the major aspects of American life . . . systematic analysis led to the one factor that consistently and dramatically affects the values and behavior of Americans. This factor is the level of religious commitment. . . . This force is rapidly becoming a more powerful factor in American life than whether someone is liberal or conservative, male or female, young or old, or a blue-collar or white-collar worker.[2]

The researchers did not expect to reach these conclusions but the evidence was compelling.

Other studies have reached similar conclusions. A study done by the *Dayton* [Ohio] *Journal Herald* of religious beliefs and practices reported, "Various voices in the past decade have told us that we . . . have drifted from our civilization's great religious tradition. That, it turns out, was an exaggeration." This study also found that more than half of the church members claimed to have had a "born again" experience and 40 percent of the general population had done so. Forty-six percent of the people attend church weekly and another 18 percent attend several times a year.[3]

A final example of the increased interest in religion is found in data gathered by the Gallup organization. In a book entitled *The Search for America's Faith*, the aspirations of the nation's youth are described.

The young indicate that they want to go deep into the great places of God through prayer, Bible study and personal discipline. Recreational activities and entertainment are way down on the urgency scale. . . . Relevance is no longer the code word in the religious quest of youth. Get used to a new word: spirituality.[4]

The implications of this trend for the parish are obvious. Increasing numbers of people are searching for values that will give meaning and purpose to their lives. The affluence which many enjoy, the opportunities for entertainment and recreation, or the retreat into drugs do not address, much less answer, the ultimate questions.

Dealing with such matters is what religion is about. This is done within the context of the local parish. It is here that individuals struggle with such matters as the meaning and purpose of life, the understanding of death, and matters of right and wrong. It is within the parish that the people come to an understanding of God and the demands their faith places on them. It is here that the ministry of the church takes place.

The congregation that addresses these issues will be carrying out the purpose for which God has called it into existence. It will be relevant to people at their point of deepest need, that of finding meaning and purpose in life. This does not mean that the church should not give attention to matters which can improve the quality of this life—matters such as justice, peace, liberation, and material welfare. However, unless the spiritual needs and values are addressed, all the rest will, in the final analysis, be meaningless, akin to the man who gained the whole world but lost his soul.

CONCLUSION

If space permitted, I could list several other factors that are having an impact on the parish, things like the continual reorganizations which have been going on in several denominations (United Methodists call it restructure). This consumes time and energy and gives the illusion of progress. The local people barely learn the new nomenclature and procedures before they are changed again.

Fortunately the parish is a tough organization. It continues to survive and serve in spite of what we do to it. The denomination may be able to enhance the work of the local church or to make that work more difficult, but the ministry of the local congregation continues.

The parish is as important today as it has ever been. The rapid technological and social changes we have witnessed in our lifetime have not lessened its significance. If anything, these have made the parish even more important. In a world which is experiencing rapid change, people need to hear the word from God, to know there are some things which are beyond the instability and transience of life, some things which transcend time. It is within the parish that they hear this word and are nurtured and grow in the faith. It is here that individuals find the supportive community with whom they share life's joys and sorrows, its triumphs and defeats. It is within this context that persons form the values by which they live and which give life meaning. Finally, the parish provides the motivation and the structure by which people serve. These include service not only in the local congregation and community but the means by which members contribute to the worldwide mission of the church.

The parish has been and will continue to be the basic unit for the proclamation of the gospel and the nurture of people in the Christian faith. The external environment will continue to change. The denominations will design different structures and procedures. But the parish will continue to be a place where the love of God is made manifest. It will continue to be a place where people worship and serve God by showing love to others. The parish which sees this as its task will fulfill the role for which God has called it into being and will continue to do so despite changes which may occur in the society and in the denomination.

1. "The Nation's Values—Still Alive," *U.S. News and World Report*, July 5, 1982, p. 47.
2. *The Connecticut Mutual Life Report on American Values in the '80s: The Impact of Belief,* 1981, p. 6.
3. *Durham Morning Herald*, January 23, 1982.
4. George Gallup, Jr. and David Poling, *The Search for America's Faith* (Nashville: Abingdon, 1960), p. 34.

Chapter 6

Our Missional Constituencies: Unchurched, Unconnected, and Unknown

René O. Bideaux

There is another dimension to our evangelistic task which has been only marginally considered. I refer to the people, the constituencies to whom and with whom we are called to proclaim the good news of God's disclosure in Jesus Christ. It is interesting how frequently the significant events and teachings in Jesus' life (at least as reported by the evangelists) revolved around an imagery or setting of banquets and meals. I believe this can help us clarify, in part, the meaning of the church's God-given mission. We might look at the feeding of the multitude, the meal with the tax collector, the last supper with the disciples, or the wedding banquet. But, for the purpose of considering the diverse constituencies that are central to the mission of God's church today, I will be focusing our attention on the Great Banquet.

When we concern ourselves with evangelism and church growth, when we affirm that each local church is to be a center of mission, we must recognize that in each moment and place in history there will be specific and unique people in whom and through whom God calls the church to be responsive and to reach out. *My thesis* is that there is growth and extension in Christ's church when and where it turns to the missional constituencies of its time and place in history.

I pray you will allow me some license in the use of the Great Banquet. In referring to the parable of the Lord of the banquet, I find a very helpful typology for understanding those special constituencies that claim North American Methodism today. For our purpose they are the unchurched (I include the underchurched), the unconnected, and the unknown.

THE PARABLE OF THE GREAT BANQUET

The Parable of the Great Banquet reads as follows:

Jesus answered, "A man was giving a big dinner party and had sent out many invitations. At dinnertime he sent his servant with a message for his guests, 'Please come, everything is now ready.' They began one and all to excuse themselves. The first said, 'I have bought a piece of land, and I must go and look over it; please accept my apologies.' The second said, 'I have bought five yoke of oxen, and I am on my way to try them out; please accept my apologies.' The next said, 'I have just got married and for that reason I cannot come.' When the servant came back he reported this to his master. The master of the house was angry and said to him, 'Go out quickly into the street and alleys of the town, and bring me in the poor, the crippled, the blind, and the lame.' The servant said, 'Sir, your orders have been carried out and there is still room.' The master replied, 'Go out on to the highways and along the hedgerows and make them come in; I want my house to be full.' I tell you that not one of those who were invited shall taste my banquet." (Luke 14:16-24, NEB)

This same story appears in a slightly different form in Matthew in order to point up the moral rightness of Jewish wars. Here Luke seems to be concerned with the response of Jesus' Jewish contemporaries. Jesus is saying that those in society, whom the Jews may despise as sinners and outcasts, will enter the kingdom of God.

What impresses me about the parable is how God's love is portrayed as leaping over the barriers of status, nationality, and race. Neither poverty, nor ignorance, nor sin can exclude God's grace. There are three constituencies that receive specific attention from the Lord of the banquet.

First, the servant is sent to the "invited" guests to tell them that the banquet is ready. Jesus and his disciples went first to the Jews, but few responded. A piece of land, a yoke of oxen, a new wife—the guests had the same secular excuses then as do too many today: possessions, the means of a livelihood, and personal relationships. Such legitimate concerns become forms of idolatry and pride when they stand in the way of responding to the claim that God places on us. The invited guests were clearly knowledgeable of the promises God had made. They were trained in the temple schools. The scriptural promises they had heard, but few responded.

Second, the Lord of the banquet sent his servant into the streets and alleys of the town. He was told to collect the poor, the crippled, the blind, and the lame. There is room for all. These were the common people of the land. Many had neglected the law or were ritually unclean persons.

Finally, the Lord of the banquet sent his servant into the highways and along the hedgerows. He wanted a full table. This was the wider Gentile world into which the early church was moved to venture. The banquet table had space for all who would respond to the summons.

These three groupings are very much present in our world today and mark the missional constituencies with which and toward whom the church must direct its attention. Whether proclaiming the good news, inviting to discipleship, or loosening the bonds of oppression, God claims our faithfulness among those in society who have borne the mark of their Redeemer, among those who stand outside society's mainstream, and among those who seemingly stand over against our society and culture. There is a place at the great banquet table for all who will respond.

THE UNCHURCHED

One of the most significant phenomena in North America has been the shift or movement of large populations into what is known as the Sunbelt of the United States. In Florida the population increased nearly 44 percent between 1970 and 1980, while the national population increased only 11 percent. But Florida does not represent the highest rate of increase. In the Southwest, population totals advanced 46 percent over the same period of time.

For the total fifteen-state area identified as the Sunbelt, population increases were double the national figures for the ten-year, 1970-1980 period: 68 million to 83 million. This leads to the question of what happened to United Methodist membership. In Florida, United Methodism grew 8 percent over against a population increase of 44 percent. In the fifteen-state Sunbelt region our United Methodist membership declined 5 percent while the region increased its population 22 percent.

The above data only suggest that Methodists are not reaching their shifting unchurched and underchurched population. In part, these populations are the baptized or confirmed members who have moved and become nonparticipants in the church of their birth. They received their invitations some time in the past, as it were. We are concerned here about a great many individuals who may never have become official "members" of a local church but who were raised in the church and have heard the good news and many have been in the fellowship. Many have been tagged for invitations; they just haven't publicly accepted the invitation. The unchurched, such as these, are all around us, not just in the Sunbelt, and they are increasing. The church's most obvious missional constituency is made up of these whom the Lord of the banquet called the "invited."

We know, just as Jesus did, what keeps the "invited" away from the church: power, idolatry, and pride. The worship of possessions, vocations, and relationships leads to excuses that separate the "invited" from God. To be faithful is first to call those already invited, the unchurched, to the banquet table of the Lord.

THE UNCONNECTED

We used to have a clothesline at home. My job was to string it. I had to place a loop or hitch in the line over each hook so the line was connected from hook to hook. If I skipped or could not reach a hook, the line would become disconnected rather readily. So the church must maintain a direct connection with the real world of people or it becomes disconnected. I'm afraid we Methodists may be increasingly unconnected from the majority of people in the streets and alleys of our cities and communities. Our social, economic, and educational levels have risen so high that it's almost impossible to attach the "clothesline."

The "unconnected" in our world are everywhere; they may be abused women and children, the aged, the maimed and the lame, the exile or refugee, the homosexual, the blind and sick, the economically poor. We pass by unconnected people daily. The primary characteristic of their lives is a sense of powerlessness and disconnectedness. They find themselves out of the mainstream of life, on the margins, unable to fully control or direct their lives, often experiencing oppression and injustice.

Current statistics show that in the United States somewhere around 1.8 million women are battered every year. One such violent incident is reported each minute. The abused woman stands in a terrifying and isolated situation. Add to this the abuse of children, physically and sexually, the experience of divorce or death of a spouse. These are all unconnected or unconnecting experiences.

What is the mission of the church? What is the good news of Jesus Christ for these persons?

Another area of unconnectedness in North America has resulted from dramatic economic shifts in the past two decades. Unemployment has been in double digits. Here in the United States reductions in the food stamp, nutrition, and health benefit programs have cast millions into the category of the chronically poor. In Los Angeles some Salvadoran refugees have been known to survive on banana peels and live in abandoned cars. The unemployed, the hungry, and many refugees must live out their lives below the minimal levels of necessity in our societies. These are the unconnected. Today, our churches have relatively few of these persons within their membership. As the servants of the Lord of the banquet, we are challenged to reach out to these with the same grace that God has extended to us.

One further example of the disconnected in America are those who have been and are being removed from the land by increased corporate control of the resources and means of production. This is dramatically illustrated in the removal of black families from land ownership in the United States. In eleven southern states blacks owned 16 million acres of farm land in 1910. This fell to 6 million in 1970, and 2 million in 1980. In Mississippi, black-owned farms represented 54 percent of all farms (28 percent of the acreage) in 1935. In 1978, this had decreased to 8 percent of the farms and less than 10 percent of the land. Recent studies in Appalachia demonstrate how the poor white people there have also lost control of the land to large corporations. Do these people attend our churches when they move in desperation to the cities?

When we turn to the streets and alleys to invite persons to our Lord's banquet table, we are extending the saving hope of Christ to the ones Jesus referred to so often as the sick and blind, the lame and imprisoned, women and children, the aged and poor. All who are disconnected from life and powerless to change or control the conditions of their lives are our missional constituency, just as much as the already invited.

THE UNKNOWN

The unknown, to whom the servants of the Lord are sent in

mission today, are persons in our midst of different races, languages, customs, and histories. As Methodists, I would suggest we are generally unacquainted with these constituencies in North America. An illustration of how uninformed most United Methodists are can be noted in the stereotyping of Asian Americans as being a "model minority." A speaker, addressing the National Federation of Asian American United Methodists, identified this attitude most clearly: "They behave; they are quiet, industrious; and they have improved themselves." This perception is racist, breeds division among ethnic minorities, and is ultimately used to manipulate and control non-Asian Americans. It demonstrates how unacquainted most Methodists are with regard to just this one ethnic group.

Such a stereotype overlooks sweatshops and poverty; it is blind to unemployment and underemployment, high rates of disease and suicide—all of which are intimate parts of the Asian American experience. The 1970 census set the Asian American population at 1.5 million. This excluded 350,000 Southeast and Pacific Island people and all the Indochina refugees. Since 1970 the population of Asian Americans has grown to exceed 3,000,000. Koreans have increased nearly 500 percent and Filipinos, the largest Asian American cultural group in the United States, have increased nearly 150 percent in these ten years. Do we really know these Asian Americans?

Similar insights can be shared about native populations, especially as we begin to identify the large hidden populations in our urban centers. The Spanish-speaking communities are the fastest growing unknown missional constituency for The Methodist Church. As Methodists we think we are acquainted with the black community. This is a fantasized deception for United Methodists. When we act on such fantasies, the results can be damaging to persons and certainly discouraging to their inclusion in the local church.

The needs, concerns, histories, and possibilities of the unknown people in the byways and hedges of our lives are legion for most Methodists in North America. Unfortunately, even less understood are the local church background and religious experiences of these persons. The issue is, How do we become faithful in proclaiming the good news to them, especially when much of North American Methodism is disconnected from and unknowing of the most rapidly growing constituencies in our midst?

STRATEGIES/IMPLICATIONS

I want to isolate a few brief suggestions for strategies to help the Methodist churches of North America in the missional task of evangelism at all levels: the local church, the conference, and the general church. I believe we can and will reach out and proclaim the good news to all God's creation.

The three typologies or categories of constituencies (unchurched, unconnected, and unknown) are obviously not mutually exclusive. They represent three categories of people in North America. Each requires different strategies if we are to proclaim the good news in its fullness "to the poor—of release for prisoners—of recovery of sight for the blind—to let the broken victims go free—and to proclaim the year of the Lord's favor" (Luke 4:18-19, NEB). It is not as though the rapidly growing Spanish-speaking communities in America, for example, might not be unchurched, unconnected, and unknown by our predominantly white middle-class Anglo local churches. The chances are very good that Spanish-speaking constituencies will be found in all three of these relationships with the majority and dominant church, especially in the United States and Canada.

Some of the strategies I wish to suggest have already been mentioned. My intention is simply to illustrate possible directions as a means of focusing more specifically on the God-originating claim that addresses the Methodist church today. I will lift up seven strategies or emphases:

(1) The development of *missional congregations* is our goal. By definition this is what it means to be the church. There are certain characteristics which such congregations will demonstrate: the commitment to propagate the gospel, the commitment to self-support, the commitment to self-direction, the commitment to serve others as much as or more than self.

(2) We need to focus on the intentional and strategic deployment of *missionary personnel*. We recognize that trained leadership is lacking in the areas of new church development, congregational revitalization, and the supervision of young pastors in these ministries. We must consider deploying more missionary personnel in North America. I would suggest these might come from two sources: within our own denominations and from churches representing the language and racial/nationality constituencies. One of

the exciting new developments in United Methodism is the arrival of Korean missionaries, deployed by the Korean church to the United States. The United States will be the "object" of their ministries. Also, preliminary talks have taken place with the Methodists of the Caribbean to possibly help with proclaiming the good news to Caribbean immigrants in the United States. The use of missionary personnel will be necessary if we are to really construct and transverse bridges with the "unconnected" and "unknown."

(3) High priority must be given to the mobilization of the *local church*. There is no doubt that the local congregation continues to be the center of Christian mission for Methodism. Programs for sister or brother partnerships in mission are already in place within The United Methodist Church. These must be strengthened and expanded. Cooperative parishes already have demonstrated their ability to establish new congregations. Such multi-church endeavors promise much. Also, the use of volunteers is a burgeoning reality in the church. We must focus these to more energetic commitment within North America.

(4) *Existing congregations* must be seen in some areas as viable foundations for establishing essentially new congregations. Revitalization and renewal, even replacement and closure, can take place. More often than not, we have the skills but lack the will.

(5) *Finance and field services* provided mainly for capital fundraising campaigns can become comprehensive. I envision a corps of highly experienced field staff who covenant with a district or conference to shepherd a young minister (it will be a while before our seminaries train up a class of specialists) "from beginning to end" in the establishment of a new congregation. These services are in place. We need a commitment to the task and a way of packaging these services.

(6) Our denomination's many *institutional ministries*, especially where related to serving the unconnected and unknown, can become points for the establishment of new congregations among these constituencies. We have examples of this, but we have not intentionally planned for it.

(7) Models for less capital-intensive congregational life must be

discovered for new church development. We are secure denominations. We enjoy the comforts of material possessions and well-paying professional ministries that serve our congregations. This lifestyle in the local church does not readily attract the many who stand outside the mainstream of white middle-class existence. Less capitalization and professionalization of our ministry will be essential.

CONCLUSION

There is no lack of missional constituencies with which the church must be involved. What is lacking is the will, the commitment, and the loyalty to the Lord of the banquet.

When Jesus was being entertained by one of the leading Pharisees, he said to his host: "When you give a lunch or dinner party, do not invite your friends, your brother, or other relations, or your rich neighbors; they will only ask you back again and so you will be repaid. But when you give a party, ask the poor, the crippled, the lame, and the blind; and so find happiness. For they have no means of repaying you; but you will be repaid on the day when good men rise from the dead" (Luke 14:12-14, NEB).

This picture of the poor, the crippled, the lame, and the blind reminds us again of the mission of Jesus which he outlined as he spoke in the synagogue at Nazareth ("The spirit of the Lord is upon me because he has anointed me . . ." [Luke 4:18f, NEB]). This mission is not easy. Persistence, vulnerability, compassion—these are essential ingredients.

This is the priority, the prime missional constituency for God's mission today. If God's church is faithful, it must be proclaiming, acting out, intervening, empowering all these to come to the table: the unchurched, the unconnected, and the unknown. All have a place at the banquet table. This is no simple charity. The issue is integrity—the integrity of the church of Jesus Christ. There is no church except where we are willing to seat all of these at the table of the Lord.

One of the exciting processes going on among North American Methodists is the intentional cooperation along the border between the United States and Mexico. Functioning there is a Southwest Border Consultation. Its purpose is to bring together in that clearly defined geographical area a coordinated ministry involving the cooperation of the several annual conferences of The United Methodist Church and the Evangelical Methodist Church of Mexico. This is a significant recognition of the missional constituencies in all of their dimensions of being unchurched, unconnected, and unknown.

God has truly sent us as servants "to announce good news to the poor, to proclaim release for prisoners and recovery of sight for the blind; to let the broken victims go free, to proclaim the year of the Lord's favor" (Luke 4:18-19, NEB).

Chapter 7

On the Outside Looking In: The Story of the Church Dropout And What the Church Can Do About It

Gordon Bruce Turner

The church of Jesus the Christ needs to be aware of its focus for the mission of evangelization. Indeed there are many such potential foci. I would sense, however, that few churches have sharpened that focus sufficiently to be aware of what their intentionality in evangelism is all about.

The problems in evangelism in mainline denominations are two-fold. On the one hand, evangelism has really been the church talking to itself. It is the washed washing the already washed. It is the saved talking to the saved. It is the converted trying again to convert the already convinced. That is not evangelism! Here the arrows of mission are pointing inwardly toward the church. That is the inherent problem of many crusade and television ministries. Whatever else they may be, they are not evangelism. And the second problem is like unto it. Mainline denominations, when they assume a mandate for evangelism, use the buckshot approach to the outside unsuspecting world. They aim at nothing in particular, and usually hit the same. One wise person said, "If you are aiming at nothing you will hit it every time." Such, in many cases, have been our evangelization efforts. An inwardly directed evangelism, or an outwardly unfocused evangelism, usually gains the same thing: little growth, few numbers, a few fuzzy feelings, but little credible discipleship gain for the Lord of life.

As we begin our excursions, I would like for you to take part in an experiential exercise. Those who have read some of my other writings will be aware of my "Parable of the Pond." It is one way of looking at the potential of the church community. Think of your local congregation in terms of this parable of the pond. You are standing at the edge of your favorite pond and hurl a rock into the center of it. The ripples begin to go out from that central splash in ever-widening circles. One circle builds on another until there are nine concentric circles.

These circles represent the "rings" of your church. From the center where the most active and involved people are, the circles move out to the edge where people are not involved in the church at all. We have given names to these "rings" and the pond might look something like this:

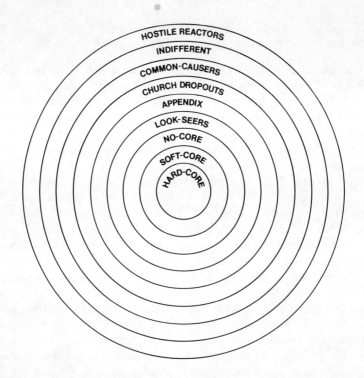

Who are these people? What do they look like? Please keep in mind that I am a Canadian pastor and theologian and my perceptions are framed within that context.

The *hard core* are those persons whom we see everywhere in the life of the church. They are involved in leadership in multiple ways. They are at worship most of the time. They can be depended upon to do anything and everything. And what's more, when they make a financial pledge, they keep it fully, and for good measure they add 10 percent. They represent about 15 percent of our church family membership list.

The *soft core* are regulars too. They attend over 60 percent of the worship services, are involved in some committees and they come when they can. They help when it's convenient. That basement floor that needs painting so the Guides/Scouts won't get skinned knees—they'll do it Saturday if it doesn't interfere with their golf or curling. They pledge and will pay about 80 percent of what they pledge. This "soft core" represents about 70 percent of our church population.

The *no-core* are those people who come rarely or occasionally. We see them at Easter, Christmas, baptisms, weddings, and funerals. They call the church "their church," but we would never know it by their attendance or involvement. And just try removing them from your membership lists! Actually, some of them contribute a significant part to the budget. However, they tell us they don't feel the need to be part of the worshiping fellowship. Perhaps they do get all they need in their occasional excursions into the life of the church. They represent another 10 percent of our church folk.

The *look-seers* are in the gallery looking in. They are with us once in a while. They are curious about "who we are as the people of God." They wonder if we are who we say we are, and whether this Christ we talk about has anything relevant to say to them. They are curious, just looking occasionally.

The *appendix* is that group of people we have moved from our membership lists to a list of "those who used to be." Some churches remove them after they have not been to Holy Communion for over three years. I have never quite understood why that was the one mark of a person's spirituality. In some cases they are like our biological appendix. They can cause us problems or pain and so we tend to get rid of them rather than rectifying the situation.

The *church dropout* is a technical term for those persons who evidence the following marks:

- They never attend worship, although they once did.
- They are involved in no church-related activities, although they used to be.
- They give no financial support to the church.
- They have a negative attitude toward the church they used to attend.
- Their decision to leave the local church was marked by pain (a pain they can still identify at some level).
- They can still talk about faith issues in a convincing way and their private lives may still be marked by traditional pietism, such as prayer and Bible reading.

67

- They are "believers but not belongers."

These people have voted with their feet and their pocketbooks in rejecting the local churches of which they used to be an active part.

The *common-causers* are those people who colleague with church folk in many important local church projects. They participate with us in forming day-nursery schools, self-help education programs for the unemployed, and lobbies concerning political issues. They worked with us in the civil rights movement and are currently partnered with the church in the peace movement. They think church folk are "neat people." They like us, but they don't believe in our Christ or want to be part of his Body.

The *indifferent* do not think what we feel or believe is important, or is of value to their lives. They give the gospel and the church a big yawn. Christian faith is a non-issue. As far as they are concerned, the church doesn't do much good in society, and probably doesn't do much harm either.

The *hostile reactors* are marked by their opposition to the church. They have an adversarial stance to the people of God. Some of them hold that stance for good reasons. Church history does have some blots on its rearview mirror.

Now at this point let me declare that I have a particular bias for the focus of evangelization. It is the church dropout. Partly, it is because I have many friends in that category for whom I covet the meaning of the gospel and wish the excitement and vibrancy of kingdom living. But also it is because, in the fishing pond of the church's potential community, they represent millions of potential disciples who are on the outside looking in. They were once *us;* they are now *them.*

The United Church of Canada is but one mainline denomination which has suffered the 10 percent people drain. It has watched its life's blood go from its arteries and veins, sapping its strength for ministry in the Canadian community and nation. Membership, one of the most widely used barometers of vitality and health, has declined the 10 percent which has afflicted almost all mainline churches in the USA and Canada. In 1965, the United Church of Canada reached its highpoint of church membership. It listed 1,064,033 persons as members. The decline began gradually, but then the internal bleeding became a stream in the 1970s. By 1977, membership had plummeted to 930,226. 1980 indicated a registration of 903,302. In the last full year (1982) for which statistics are available, we still show a 9 percent decline.

Since most of the mainline denominations have contributed with equal generosity to the church dropout pool, one can see that pool as a rich assemblage for engagement in discipling. And it keeps growing. I believe it to be one of the most significant areas for the current focus on evangelism. Research indicates that many people in new church development areas have been and are church dropouts.

WHO ARE THE CHURCH DROPOUTS?

But who are these church dropouts? What has been their story, inside and outside the church? From the perspective of the outsider looking in, what can they tell the chuch? I would like for us to look through the eyes of particular people in a particular setting at a particular time. They do not tell us all there is to know about the dropout. They cannot be generalized into broad principles. But they might give us some hunches, some sensitivities, into the lives of the people we know who are church dropouts. They might even give us an understanding of the preventative medicine needed to stem the "backdoor flood" of the church people in our own part of the vineyard.

The names of all persons and families have been changed. Their confidentiality has been honored insofar as that has been possible. However, they all were people who dropped out of the life of the church in the fifteen-year period prior to 1972.

The story of this church is an interesting one. It began as a country charge outside a major city. Gradually the city expanded so that the church was at the center of a booming suburban development. Excited church folk voted for a new church building, and they built it large. After all, soon there would be flocks of people to be cared for. Sadly, however, the church never did grow that much. It remained at a membership of 500 to 700 for many years.

People began to ask *why*. The community had grown, why didn't the church? Attendance seemed to have settled in at about 300 and they had built a sanctuary to seat up to 700. The *why* questions began to surface in the stories of individual people. "You remember Mrs. Jones? She used to be so active here—in the United Church women, the Friendly Circle, the pot lucks. Never see her around here anymore, though. Sometimes I see her at the grocery store, but never at church. I wonder why?" And, "You should have known Bill Smith. What a tower of strength he was a few years ago. He was one of the stewards, a trustee, and the painter par excellence in the old hall. He even led the Scouts. We often wondered when he had time for his family. He was at the church so much. But he's not at church now. We don't know why."

Stories like these encouraged me to begin journeying with the church dropouts who were still in the community. It was a year of fascinating conversations and analysis. It became the basis of a doctoral thesis entitled "Pastoral Conversation with the Church Dropout." The thesis focused on the relationship between pastoral care and evangelism. When these are seen in their caricatures—which ultimately leads to simplistic understandings and falsifications—they are generally held to be incompatible. An evangelist may not give adequate pastoral care because of an overshadowing concern for a yes to the gospel. Likewise, the pastoral care-giver may never come close to gaining such a yes.

In conversations with these church dropouts I came to the conviction that the task of giving attention to the needs of people (the pastoral care function) need not be inherently incompatible with the responsibility of sharing the claims of the gospel or inviting people to reconsider their commitment to Christ and the church. It is part of a holistic view of evangelical ministry.

The following chart identifies some reasons these families left the church.

Percentage	Number of Cases	Identified Reasons
36	9	Church not meeting personal needs
0	0	Loss of confidence in the church
12	3	Inadequate ministry in times of crisis
8	2	Conflict with pastor or church member
0	0	Theological conflicts
8	2	Crisis of faith
36	9	Change of lifestyle
100%	25	

Behind these statistics are the stories of persons who were once active church members. It might be helpful to hear some of these stories.

Nine case studies represented persons who became church dropouts because the church was not meeting their personal needs. These persons are representative of a number of concerns that are seen in the life of the church. In many cases these issues and concerns can be appropriately addressed by the church. Some represent false ideas of what the church is to be and to do in the world.

One family stated that the church is in the business of helping people get prepared for living. When young people are prepared for life and feel that they no longer need the church to prepare them for mature living, then it seems appropriate that they should leave. Thus, as the youngest child in this family completed Sunday school and was subsequently confirmed, the family saw no need for further church involvement. "We just didn't go back to church the fall after Jennie was confirmed. There didn't seem to be any point. We didn't need to any more." Thus, confirmation had served as convenient graduation "out of church." So often it serves as that. The church is a nurturing agency in life. It does prepare people for living. But preparation is an ongoing commitment for Christians, and graduation isn't at confirmation time. Confirming one's baptismal vows is but another step in the unfolding journey of Christian discipleship.

No matter how we feel about the inappropriateness of this family's conviction, it remains true for them. We can have deep regrets that they see the church for what they can get out of it rather than what they can put into it. It is, from our perspective, sad that they see ministry as directed *to* them rather than seeing themselves as being part of the people of God in ministry to a world in need.

They look back at their experience of the church with no negative feelings. "Great people," they say, "we liked them." It is also of interest that their children, now grown to adulthood, confirm their parents' visions of the church. They say, "Sure, we'll come back to church when we have kids and they need Sunday school." And when pressed a bit further, "Yes, we'll probably leave too when they're out of Sunday school." This is a limited view of the church, lacking much of the vision of Christ. However, there are many persons like these in the church dropout population.

Another young married woman became indifferent to the church because it did not meet her needs for fellowship and warmth. She grew up in a small country church. There, people knew her well and cared for her deeply. She could call everyone by name. She then moved to a large, impersonal suburban area. It was easy to go to church and have no one call you by your first name. She didn't feel part of the family of God in worship. The women's groups didn't meet her needs for affiliation. Gradually, she drifted out of the

71

church. Because there were no small congregations nearby, she became a "believer but not a belonger."

A significant proportion in this category represents people who question the church's lack of prophetic witness in a confusing world. One put it bluntly: "The church doesn't have the guts to deal with this messed up world." Story after story relates how people came to church expecting something relevant for life. Life was not easy. They had questions. The signs of the times were confusing and demanded a "word of the Lord." Yet the pulpit remained strangely silent. They expected the word of God to meet the places where life ached and needed most to be questioned. Hence they saw the church slipping into irrelevance.

Quite clearly the church has a prophetic role in our society. The myth that the pulpit concerned with social issues will empty the pews is just that—a myth. People expect a word from the Lord which addresses real life. The Bible and the daily newspaper need to talk with each other in a prophetic ministry for our time.

A second high percentage of people left the church because of a change in lifestyle. These were of two categories. Because the community is on the fringe of a highly popular resort area in Canada, many people moved into a new leisure style of living. It is also an affluent community. Hence, most people could afford it. Thus, many of the people were absent from the church from May until October. It is a simple step to lengthen that period to a full year as cottages were winterized. Faith can then easily move to the periphery of life when it is not fed by the nurture of regular worship and church involvement. A second change in lifestyle characterized those who moved to a different category of life. For some it was widowhood. For others it was becoming a single parent. For some it was the mobility of vocation. As they moved higher up the ladder of management responsibility, or down it, the church developed a new relevance or nonrelevance.

The church, with rare exceptions, has not learned to deal with the changing lifestyles of people. It is focused on the family as it used to be. Single people don't crowd its doors. Those who are single or who have become single again are not sure where they fit. The increasing demands of a leisure society have slammed the ball in the court of the church for some innovative and creative ministry in times of crisis. Yet that is probably inevitable when we allow ministry to be perceived solely as the responsibility of the ordained. Pastors, too, have glaring weaknesses in their gifts for ministry.

Until we are able to build on the gifts of all the people of God and see pastoral ministry as everyone's ministry, it is likely that the crises of many will be inadequately handled.

Three families became church dropouts during times of family bereavement. One told of a pastor who never came back to deal with their grief and bewilderment after the funeral. This was repeated in all three family cases, and it forced these people outside the church to do their questioning and crying. They stood outside the church looking in. They blamed others for the deaths, then themselves, and finally God. Neither the pastor nor the people shared in the journey of their grief.

Some people left the church because of conflict with the pastor or a church member. Conflicts do happen; and some conflicts should happen. There is an offense to the gospel. But when the offense of the gospel and the compassion of Christ for people are not held in tension in the same encounter, people drift out of the church feeling rejected.

A crisis of faith also happens for people when what they sincerely believe and what life presents them do not match. When belief and reality are not compatible, something gives way in thinking-believing structures. One delightful person told the story of a parent's horrendous death. She was a firm Christian and watched her father die, inch by inch. The parent also was a believing Christian who talked on his deathbed about a "loving God." With as much conviction as she could muster, she told me, "That's just not true!" The fiber of faith in her life rotted away gradually when she couldn't hold together a "loving God" who seemed incapable of helping her own father.

Strangely enough, no people left because of a lack of confidence in the church as an institution. It remained for them a valued agency in society. They would not want to live in a community without churches. It had its place, but not currently for them. Neither did any leave because of theological conflicts. What the church taught and what they believed were not in tension. The church had not forced them out by what it publicly said. These categories in other research have often been much higher, but for this population they were nonexistent.

HELPING THE CHURCH DROPOUT

Our objective was not merely to identify the church dropout but to address what the church might do about the problem. The church as a community of faith and as caring persons bears a responsibility for initiating that which enables the dropout to find his or her way back. People often leave the church for reasons unrelated to the body they leave. But if the church is concerned for persons, it needs to engage whatever impinges itself upon the lives of all of God's children.

There is, or can be, a definite relationship between evangelism and pastoral care. Pastoral care leads to growth and fàith (what we call evangelization) when the following six phases have been significantly touched in the course of the conversational life between the care-giver/evangelizer and the dropout.

- The pastoral base
- Attentiveness to existing needs
- The mutuality of searching
- Growth through existential sharing
- The power of suggestion
- The claim of decision

These phases of conversation are not always sequential. It is often a bit like two steps forward and one back on the venture of evangelization. You spend some time *deepening the pastoral base and being attentive to whatever needs present themselves.* You move ahead to some sharing in a mutual way, and then you find yourself back on the first plane again. That's the way the journey of evangelism seems to be. It looks a bit like the stairway on the following page.

I use the stairway illustration deliberately. It is necessarily an advancement upward and outward rather than downward and inward. The spiritual journey moves toward the peaks of spiritual experience and encountering God who is beyond. God is to be found not only within, but beyond oneself. Journeying, for the Christian, is not simply an inward pathway of meditation, but of reaching out beyond oneself.

I would like to turn to the importance of each of these phases. First, there is the *pastoral base.* Fundamental to every growth in the ownership of faith is the existence of an adequate pastoral base. At its simplest, this phase refers to being attentive to the life situation of the other. Just prior to my working with Sewart Hiltner at Princeton, he had published *Ferment in the Ministry.* In his own way he portrayed the clergy's function in different categories and then presented a new image of current possibilities. I used his depiction of

74

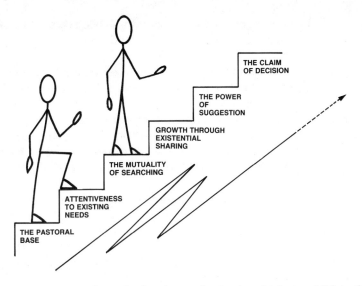

THE CLAIM
OF DECISION

THE POWER
OF
SUGGESTION

GROWTH THROUGH
EXISTENTIAL
SHARING

THE MUTUALITY
OF SEARCHING

ATTENTIVENESS
TO EXISTING
NEEDS

THE PASTORAL
BASE

the shepherd tending the lamb caught in the thickets of life—the shepherd using all the modern skills available. This is the base from which we begin. The picture portrays what all pastoral theologians have pointed to in terms of the importance of the accepting-under-standing-reflecting-clarifying-integrating continuum for pastoral presence.

It is important if the conversation is to move upward and outward that the care-giver/evangelist be *attentive to existing needs*. Where needs are openly and honestly dealt with, the other person is receptive to letting the pastor begin the process of sharing his or her own faith. Needs must be acknowledged and dealt with, though not always met. If one rides roughshod over another's needs, or fails to recognize them, in almost every case the opportunity for evangelism is lost. Faith is not nurtured for growth.

Marlene was a dropout who made great strides in the development of her faith over a four-month period of conversations. I referred to her earlier as one who left during a crisis of faith. Her father's death brought her to an impasse. She had to deal with unresolved grief. This exhibited itself in a number of emotional and physical symptoms.

> *Mr. T:*   This was your first experience with any emotional diffi-
> culty?
> *Marlene:* Well, the only kind of emotional difficulty I ever had had

been with my mother . . . and that's been during the last few years . . . since my father died.

Mr. T: Your father died recently, then?

Marlene: Yes. About five years ago. And after he died everything seemed to fall apart. My dad and I were very close. He was my best friend.

Mr. T: That's quite a compliment for your father.

Marlene: Well, yes. But he was my best friend. But you know my father . . . *(pause)*. He was a good man. He was the best friend I ever had and life dealt him so many terrible deals.

Marlene also reflected on her relationship with her mother at this point. She indicated that her mother "made me feel guilty—up to here." She accompanied this statement by gesturing with her hands and squeezing her neck. One could quickly recognize the grief and its overwhelming power over Marlene. The attachment she still had to her father indicated her unwillingness to let him go at death. Her need was to deal with a still-present and crippling grief.

The dialogue from that first interview shows the need to allow her to talk about her grief and to identify the anger she still felt toward God for her father's death. It was the "terrible deals" of her father's illness and eventual death which led to her inability to identify a good God with the tragedy she experienced. The primary need in her life had to be dealt with. That was a need to let her identify the connections between her grief and her theology, which resulted in a crisis of faith for her. If the first interview had been such as to challenge her world view, her theological framework, or her residual grief, the flow of conversation would likely have gone nowhere. Had I noted that her view of her father was either romantic or infantile she would have probably turned her anger toward me or the church and become more deeply entrenched in her agnosticism. Had I simply replied with a simple "uh huh," I suspect that we would not have made significant gains later on. She would have been allowed to continue where she was. The process of following her feelings a little deeper in terms of her needs, with continuing support, helped her toward some new degree of freedom from her anger, guilt, and grief. Attention to her existing needs, and a clear identification of them, helped us toward the support and commitment inherent in evangelism.

There is something basic to the third phase of conversation which involves the *mutuality of searching*. Indeed there is a biblical model

76

central to its importance. In the eighth chapter of Acts, Philip the Evangelist and the Ethiopian eunuch begin to make the journey of discipleship a joint one only when the Ethiopian invites Philip to climb aboard his chariot. It is not inconsequential that Philip "began where he was" and not where he wished him to be—a common error of many evangelizers.

Faith-sharing is a mutual search. Two are in the chariot searching out the meaning of life. There is indeed bread to be found and the evangelist is bold enough to affirm that Jesus is the Bread of Life. The evangelist affirms that she/he has at least tasted the crumbs from the banquet table of the Lord of life.

It was a life-transforming event when I discovered that my life was part of the ongoing story of God. To know that we are part of God's history-making, even as Peter and Paul and Christ, is to find one's fuller liberation as a servant of God. Essentially, this is what *growth through existential sharing* is all about.

Church dropouts can begin to make some gains when the faith story that is uniquely theirs and the faith story that is uniquely that of the care-giver/evangelist intersect. Indeed, the care-giver/evangelist is also enriched in the faith. The honesty of the journey, made mutual at that time, allows for the liberation of seeing possibilities in the story of another. One's journey can be experienced through another person in a way that the solitary walk does not allow.

It is legitimate, therefore, to share one's own life journey. It it not spiritual exhibitionism but an honest revelation of one's Christian experience. It is always story-centered.

A further conversation with Marlene helps one to recognize that in the life of the evangelist (my own life) there is also pain and difficulty, a pain that can move on toward healing.

Mr. T: I see . . . you seem to feel that if one believes in God everything will turn out allright, and that our lives should be success stories.

Marlene: Well, isn't that the way it's supposed to be?

Mr. T: Well . . . I remember the funeral of one of my closest friends. He was a classmate of mine who died of brain cancer. I watched him die bit-by-bit in the hospital. It was a horrible experience.

Marlene: I remember hearing about that. He was apparently a fine man.

Mr. T: Yes, one of the best.

Marlene: Do you have a daughter?

Mr. T: Yes, I have a three-year-old daughter.

Marlene: Oh, that's nice. Do you have other children?

Mr. T: Yes. We have an eleven-year-old son.

Marlene: Oh, there's eight years between them *(pause).*

Mr. T: We had another child in between who died at birth. That was pretty difficult for us to accept and to live with. As a matter of fact, there was a long time when I felt some of the thoughts you feel about God—anger and bitterness and fear. I think it's pretty understandable that we feel that way.

Marlene: Well, I'm not sure we should talk about it very much. I feel guilty talking about my mother the way I have been. I haven't shared that with many people before—I guess with hardly anyone. I guess only my husband knows how I really feel about my mother. The doctors told me I should be able to talk to my friends or someone about what's really down deep.

Mr. T: Well, it's important to talk about our feelings. And I think it's important also to talk in the church about the feelings we have about God.

My articulation of some anger and bitterness toward God didn't make Marlene all that comfortable at first. She went on to indicate that the thoughts she felt most guilty about had to do with her relationship with her mother. A few moments later I re-emphasized that it was okay to talk in negative terms about God. She had previously, and would again, return to her angry thoughts about God but now with the assurance that it was permissible in our relationship.

The power of suggestion has become for me a sacred possession in the stewardship of the care-giver/evangelist. It is not advice-giving. Generally speaking, people don't care to hear what you are offering by way of advice. What surprised me was that when the first four phases had been touched, the power of suggestion could indeed become powerful! If one earned credibility in the pastoral relationship, one could help the other "own" the faith (or decision) he or she was pursuing by merely giving permission to reach out and affirm it. Clearly, the journey toward an "owned faith" is easier when it is mutual, and when it is pursued in the context of a warm, supporting, caring, and yet challenging partnership.

78

Again we turn to the story of Marlene. She did not really know why she had lost faith but now saw it as central to her health and well-being. Something creative began to happen in the midst of the third interview which made this possibility evolve. She toned down her hostility toward God and began to look at faith as a credible option for her life. She was beginning in that direction.

Marlene: But how do you get out of this? How am I going to become better?

Mr. T: I'm wondering if we could talk a little more about your faith. It seems to me our faith has something to say about hope. It's one of the most important things about our Christian faith—the thing that makes a big difference.

Marlene: I guess that's true, but I don't feel very hopeful. This world isn't a very hopeful place. We live in the midst of all this mess. Like my neighbor next door dying of cancer; and you hear about children with leukemia, and all those things.

Mr. T: The real world we live in is a small world full of problems, but I wonder what you believe about how things will turn out in the end. Do you believe that things will turn out all right?

Marlene: Now you're beginning to sound like those who are always saying things are coming to an end.

Mr. T: No, I don't mean that at all. What I mean is, do you believe ultimately that God is in control?

Marlene: I don't know. I just know that things are all messed up here now and God doesn't seem to care.

I later challenged her with the question, "How much faith do you have in faith?" We were both beginning to see that she was coming out of her depression. This was reflected not only in her attitude toward God but also toward herself. The concluding comments in the final interview show a woman on the march to a new, healthier, and optimistic life. The suggestion of faith as a possible strength in her life was a crucial moment in her growth as a "faithing" person, and a healthier human being.

And finally, the *claim of decision*. Isn't that the heart of evangelism? One often thinks of evangelism in terms of decision. A person decides for or against Jesus as the Christ. A person decides to come back to church again, or to continue staying away. I sense that conversion is close to the heart of the mystery of God. I believe that God alone is the converter of persons and that we as evangelists are, at best, some sort of catalyst. Our part in the conversion process is essential, for we are the storytellers of the mysteries of God. We are the channels through whom the grace of God flows in human form. But why one says yes and another no, no one knows. I can only stand before that mystery and affirm the life-changing and life-renewing God whose Spirit is available to all.

Chapter 8

New Congregations: A Mission and in Mission

James R. Maxfield

It is imperative that the Christian church have an active program of new church development. Leaders of the Christian faith have, from the beginning, used the new church as a means of spreading the gospel and its influence. The disciples of Jesus dispersed themselves to many different regions and territories, spreading the gospel of the kingdom. They established new communities of faith. The Book of Acts tells a part of this energetic story. It describes in detail three journeys of the Apostle Paul. The purpose of these journeys was twofold: to establish communities of faith (new churches), and later to encourage these churches (revitalization of existing churches). It was Paul's intention to start these communities of faith in every major center of commerce and industry in the known world.

The Christian faith has spread to every major continent because the church has had a strategy of congregational development. That is, it has not been content to serve only those within its reach. It has been moving out to new people in new places. It has been bringing together and organizing these believers into communities of faith. These new communities have reached out to encourage others to believe, and the story has gone on.

There are those who believe that the task of new church development is completed. But it will never be completed. Perhaps our responsibility would be near an end if our population were not increasing, if people were not moving, if congregations did not lose their strength and die, and if there were not varied emphases in mission and ministry in different congregations.

Since our population is still increasing and we are moving at an ever-increasing pace, we must go where the people are. The church in the early years of North American history kept up with the frontiers. It established missions, preaching posts, Sunday schools, classes, and societies where people lived. These frontiers have now changed. For the most part, our new frontiers are the burgeoning suburbs, new cities, new towns, new ethnic populations, and

81

changing communities. In northern Pinellas County, Florida, for instance, it is projected that 200,000 new persons will come to live in the next twenty years. Such growth and change in population in many areas across North America will provide the church with great opportunities.

In some of the older communities, our churches are losing their vitality. Congregations tend to have life cycles as people do. As the sociology of these communities changes, the church loses its support and dies or experiences rebirth through reorienting itself and preparing to serve the new population. If the old church dies, it may be necessary to start a new church, perhaps using the old building as a base to serve the new residents. These communities also present the church with opportunities.

An organization cannot keep its vitality and grow, unless it opens new outlets. This is true of the church. The church is under a mandate from its Lord to go to the "ends of the earth." New churches spark new vitality. New vitality causes us to push back the horizons to new endeavors and new types of mission.

Church revitalization and new church development are dependent upon a belief in the strategic importance of the congregation as a basic form of ministry. In fact, the beginning point of any rethinking of congregational development should be an emphasis on the importance of the congregation in accomplishing the church's task. The local congregation is that community, that cell, that unit of believers serving its Lord. It nurtures faith. It proclaims the gospel which is the norm for testing our beliefs and practices. It confronts persons with the message, "Thus saith the Lord." It helps to feed the hungry, heal the sick, support the bereaved. It helps to provide shelter and clothes for the shelterless and the naked. It visits those in prison. It calls for equality and justice for all. It makes its witness for peace. The congregation is the base of support for those who are involved with all the many and varied ministries. Without strong congregations the mission of the Christian church would be in serious trouble.

Some of these congregations tend to be more self-serving than mission-oriented. Some of them are biased and prejudiced against people not like themselves. Some are almost hopelessly divided. But, if the congregation is vitally important to us, we will begin to find ways to help it accomplish its mandated mission. We live in a day of planned obsolescence, but this cannot be the story of the church. The strategy of the church must be to help the congregation find and enthusiastically work at its central task. The congregation also needs to be convinced of its own vital importance as an agent of God's mission.

If the congregation is not important and vital, why join it or why ask others to? If it is not important, why even stay in its fold or support it with time, talents, or gifts? If it is not strategic in God's mission, why launch new branches? This is certainly not the first time these questions have been asked. They are in the minds of a great number of people.

Denominations and their judicatories need a strategy for new church development. The need for a strategy calls for a board, committee, or task force to be responsible for developing a set of plans for new churches and to give guidance to the new projects. Efforts in new congregational development should be very intentional.

A denominational or judicatory strategy should have the purpose of giving guidance and direction to new church development. It should not attempt to elicit conformity in every project. A strategy which is too rigid will deter new congregational development rather than assist the effort.

A strategy should insure that adequate study and research is done before a decision is made about a new project. This decision needs to be made from data rather than hunches. The record in new church development efforts shows only fractional success. A part of the reason for our failures is that too many decisions have been made without the benefit of factual data.

Research should include: (1) location of all churches within the defined area and the effectiveness of their ministry, (2) current population, (3) percentage of residents willing to participate in a possible new congregation, and (4) population projections for the next two decades. These population projections should be obtained from several different sources, such as a planning board, utilities company, and school board.

The strategy developed by the denominational or judicatory board or committee should call for a mission design for each new church. A mission design is the development of a written plan and a set of objectives for each new congregation. It is to be a chart, a road map, which will clearly suggest objectives for the new church and will suggest ways to reach these objectives. One mission design for all the new churches of a denomination or judicatory is not adequate. It should not be assumed that all communities are alike, think alike, or experience the same needs. The Letters of Paul in the New Testament reflect differences in communities and churches. Paul was forced to recognize those differences and to help guide each church on its course. These mission designs are found in Paul's New Testament letters.

A team of persons composed of judicatory leaders, nearby pastors, and interested persons in the new community should write the mission design. This group should look upon itself as the architect for a religious institution. It is to produce a blueprint, a set of drawings, for the form and structure of the new church. It is best to develop this document before the first pastor is selected. This document will then assist in the process of the selection of the first pastor. It will also serve as a guide for a job description for the first pastor.

This document will serve as an aid in the communication process. There is often a communications gap between the judicatory leaders, the pastor, and the congregation. A mission design will insure that all involved in the process will have the same expectations. It will provide the pastor and congregation with measurable objectives and goals.

The mission design should include:

1. A brief theological statement giving purpose, meaning, and identity to the project.
2. A statement showing how this project fits into the overall denominational strategy for this area or region.
3. A list of suggested objectives and goals for the first year, such as membership, finances, etc.
4. A list of suggested programs to be offered during the first year.
5. The expected role of the pastor.
6. Identification of any social problems in the community which this congregation might address.

The design should provide for periodic evaluations with the denominational leaders being involved. At least annually, the mission design itself should be evaluated and revised to reflect the changes in the community or the congregation. Any revisions deemed necessary should be agreed upon by the denominational leaders, the pastor, and the leaders of the new church.

The most important aspect of the mission design is to give direction to the congregation in its mission. It is not enough to assume that a church will automatically understand its mission in the community and to the world. A new church cannot ignore its own needs and survive. But the mission design should help the congregation look beyond its needs to the needs of the community and the world around it. Unless the church gives priority to its missional and evangelistic efforts, it may more nearly resemble a social club than a "called out" community. A social club can have an honorable purpose, but a church has a different purpose. A church's distinctiveness is in who it is and what its mission is in the community, and most important, the One to whom it owes its existence and allegiance.

Many new churches have to struggle with identity problems. In a general way the church knows who it is, but it cannot articulate clearly and specifically what its business really is. Many new churches tackle their identity problems through working toward the construction of a building. The building should always be seen as only one of the means by which the congregation will accomplish its greater objectives. The real purpose of a mission design is to spell out in detail how this new church should accomplish its mission in its community.

Most new churches in their first years receive mission funds from other nearby churches and/or from the denomination. Because of this, they see themselves as objects of mission rather than partners in mission. This understanding is detrimental to a church's development and can be fatal.

The Christian church needs to be about the business of starting new congregations. We have no acceptable alternative if we want to assume that we will continue to serve the needs of the future. Strategizing and planning cannot be overlooked if we want to make new church development a sound program with a reasonable rate of success. The congregation should be understood to be vitally important in the church's overall mission. The denomination should do everything possible to see that these new churches understand and work on their mission.

New congregations are a mission of the greater church. They are also to be in mission, partners with the greater church, from the very beginning. The church has before it some great opportunities in the area of congregational development. Every stone should be turned to assure that churches are started with the greatest possible advantage in serving the kingdom of God and the needs of God's children.

Chapter 9

Looking to the Future: Foundational Principles For Congregational Development

Kennon L. Callahan

EFFECTIVENESS

Twelve characteristics can be identified that contribute to a local church's effectiveness. In the years to come, it is important that new congregations and present ones put these central characteristics in place. Those congregations that do so with a decisive long-range plan are most likely to be effective in mission and successful in outreach.

Now, there may be 50-100 characteristics which contribute to the effectiveness of a local congregation. During the past twenty-three years I have served as the long-range planning consultant with over 750 churches across the U.S.A. Over these years of research and consultation, twelve factors have emerged persistently as the central characteristics of effective, missional congregations.

These twelve fall into two categories: six are relational characteristics and six are functional characteristics. Generally speaking, effective congregations have nine of these twelve central characteristics. Moreover, the majority of the nine are relational rather than functional. Tragically, too many churches have concentrated on the functional rather than the relational factors that contribute to effectiveness.

My book, *Twelve Keys to an Effective Church* (Harper and Row, 1983), represents an indepth study of each of the twelve characteristics. Here, I can only outline the twelve and give a brief commentary. The relational characteristics are:

1. *Specific, concrete missional objectives.* The missional church has two or three such objectives that involve strong groupings of the congregation in mission with persons who have specific human hurts and hopes.
2. *Pastoral and lay visitation.* Though a lost art in many churches, the missional church does consequential visitation with the

86

unchurched, newcomers, constituents, and members on a weekly basis.

3. *Corporate, dynamic worship.* The weekly services are holistic in music and message, corporately planned and led by a compassionate, competent team of laity and pastor.

4. *Significant relational groupings.* Most people come to a local church looking for community. Instead, we put them on a committee. Missional churches are constantly and intentionally starting new groupings in which people discover roots, place, and belonging—sharing and caring—and a sense of family.

5. *Strong leadership resources.* Many churches train leaders to fill functional slots inside the church's program. Missional churches nurture a majority of their leaders to be relational and caring with individuals and groups in the local and regional community.

6. *Streamlined structure and solid, participatory decision making.* Missional churches plan on the basis of their strengths, hopes, and objectives. They are less preoccupied with their own needs and problems than many churches. They have a streamlined organizational structure.

Among the twelve characteristics of an effective church, the functional characteristics are:

7. *Several competent programs and activities.* Missional churches know people attract people more than programs do. Generally, they have two or three really competent programs that serve rather than use people.

8. *Open accessibility.* A physical location that is accessible in terms of major traffic patterns, and leaders who are accessible to the community are both important.

9. *High visibility.* Successful missional churches have a high degree of geographical and grapevine visibility with churched and unchurched persons in the community.

10. *Adequate parking, land, and landscaping.* As a national average, one parking space permits 1.75 persons to participate in the church. Occasionally, it may be as high as 2.5 persons per space.

11. *Adequate space and facilities.* More churches underbuild than overbuild, and thereby limit their growth. They build fixed rather than flexible structures. Missional churches build for the future, with a clear perspective that this is the eleventh,

not the first, most important characteristic. Increasingly, they take energy and debt interest issues seriously.

12. *Solid financial resources.* Missional churches know people give money to people more than to programs, purposes, or paper. Missional churches tend to put their money into people rather than property. They exercise responsible, courageous stewardship.

MISSION

Mission is more important than money, mortar, maintenance, and members. Money is important. Mortar is important. Maintenance and members are important. Mission is more important.

The survival mentality of many congregations limits their effectiveness and mission, their growth and success. We need fewer churches that are interested in survival and more churches that are interested in success. Effectiveness in mission is success. Success is effective mission. I am committed to mission for the sake of mission. Growth may be a happy by-product, but it is a by-product.

Most new congregations would be advised to develop a mission plan before they develop an architectural plan. Wherever mission is tangible, mortar will have its proper place. Wherever mission is platitudinal, mortar will gain ascendancy.

Most definitely, mortar and money follow mission. To be sure, we need a realistic appraisal of mission and money, but we need to move away from a "subrosa" preoccupation with money covered by platitudes on mission.

The mistaken notion of the 1950s was the myth that the money was in the suburbs. As a matter of fact, per capita giving among the poor and among the rural has frequently been higher than in middle class suburbs.

We need to start new congregations for the sake of mission, not for payoff. Indeed, we need to intentionally start some new congregations wherein we know there will be no payoff. To be sure, it is important that some of the new congregations we start have enough of the probability of a "by-product" of payoff to make possible our starting of those congregations wherein we intentionally and consciously know there will be no payoff. It is central and decisive that people see that we are starting new congregations for the sake of mission.

88

Further, it is important that we commit ourselves to the principle that starting new congregations is more important than starting new churches. Starting movements of people in mission is more important than starting new institutions. Launching movements of people in mission is more important than building new monuments and splendid structures.

As a matter of fact, the emphasis on the theological importance of kingdom orientation as well as the theological emphasis on mission are both ways to avoid new church development simply being the 1950s approach to starting new churches under new packaging.

The 1950s represented more of a churched culture; the 1980s represent more of an unchurched culture. Now certainly, in the 1950s some of our culture was unchurched. Likewise, in the 1980s some of our culture is churched. But, by-and-large, the sense of the 1950s was that we were more of a churched than an unchurched culture. The sense of the 1980s is that we are more of an unchurched than a churched culture.

This calls for our starting new congregations with a clear kingdom orientation and a clear sense of mission. The danger is that we will simply recapitulate under new packaging the suburban emphasis of the 1950s in new locations. Mission must be the motivation for the movement we develop in starting new congregations.

RESEARCH

Research delivers decisive diagnostic data. This is true when research is at its best. The data intervention approach to research is not the best way forward in research. That approach makes the assumption that the more data we gather, the more the data will tell us the directions in which to move. Regrettably, it is more often the case that the more data we gather, the more confused we become.

The research approach which I am convinced is important for us to use in starting new congregations is the diagnostic approach to research. The diagnostic approach focuses on those critical, strategic data components which are useful in helping us shape our directions for the future.

In a famous study some ten years ago, a major corporation in the U.S.A. analyzed the 1,500 data components it was faithfully keeping. It discovered that 50 of the 1,500 data components were, in fact, decisive and critical in shaping that major corporation's sense of direction for the future. New church development will not be bene-fited from the gathering of enormous data. New church develop-ment will benefit from the thoughtful and intentional study of strategic data components.

Demographic analysis is important, but I am against demograph-ic data shaping the direction of the church. It is important and fitting that the church call into question the demographic trends of the times. One can imagine in those early years of the Christian church how impressive the demographic data out of Rome might have been, projecting the ever-increasing expansion of the Roman empire and civilization. The early church called into question the impor-tance and value of the cultural and demographic developments of the times.

Mission analysis is more important than demographic analysis. But we are naive and foolish if we imagine that church development can be effectively accomplished apart from thoughtful research and informed demographic data.

One major denomination has invested considerable amounts of leadership and financial resources in starting new congregations. Frequently they have utilized the mother-church approach. But it would be simplistic to assume that denomination has done so in a naive way.

Rather, they have mounted massive monetary resources to fund the starting of new congregations and developed one of the most advanced information systems related to census data that is available on this continent. In fact, there are those who believe their capacities and capabilities to use census data are more advanced than those of the United States Census Bureau itself. Their national denomina-tional leadership has been extraordinarily wise in putting together the diagnostic data and the money with which to make major advances in starting new congregations in this country.

RESOURCES

In the development and deployment of resources, a healthy coop-eration-competition is better than too much coordination. Fre-quently, coordination consumes more time and resources than is useful and, at the same time, delays productive results.

In the 1920s, Alfred Sloan introduced the concept of intentional overlap in a corporation which we know today as General Motors. At the same time, another corporation introduced the concept of a tidy organizational structure. The latter corporation has nearly gone out of business while the former corporation has advanced to become one of the major corporations in the country.

This is not to suggest that we are in the business of selling cars. The church is the church and it cannot copy business practices. Rather, it is to suggest that our preoccupation with coordination has contributed to our being a stable and declining denomination in this country.

In their recent book, *In Search of Excellence: Lessons from America's Best Run Companies*, Thomas Peters and Robert Waterman identify the eight basic practices they have found to be present in America's best run companies. The first is *a bias for action*. They note that the most creative companies in this country place a strong premium on action. Indeed, these companies value and prize it so highly that chaotic action is more important than orderly inaction.

As we move forward to start new congregations we can cooperate in the training of pastors to start new congregations. We can cooperate in consultation resources. We can cooperate in the financial plans that enable new congregations to move forward.

The resources we need to mount are training resources for pastors of new congregations, and consultation resources as those new congregations develop in their first, second, and third years of existence. Massive financial resources are needed so that grants, loans, and thoughtful financial plans can be available and developed with these new congregations. We are more likely to mount these resources in major ways when boards and agencies interpret their supportive role from the perspective of a kingdom orientation and with a theological perspective of mission.

MISSIONARIES

We need more "missionaries" and fewer "professional ministers" to start new congregations. The sharing of relationships; the searching for roots, place, and belonging; the shepherding of mutual hurts and hopes—these are more helpful than functional, organizational, and institutional foci for new congregations. As we launch this movement to start new congregations, we need to avoid the double myths of programs and committees.

Abroad in the church is the myth of programs; namely, that the effective church is that church which has lots of programs for all ages and all groupings. Indeed, we have virtually come to the point where program for the sake of program has become the norm in many churches. The myth is that the more programs a church has, the more likely it is to be helpful with people. No, the more programs a church has, the faster goes the merry-go-round of activities on which the people ride. We need to see that in starting new congregations the focus should be on the relational, rather than the functional components of congregational life.

The second myth abroad in the country is the myth of committees. This assumes that the best way to help persons develop strong ownership for the life and mission of a given congregation is to see that they are actively involved on some committee. This myth grows out of an assumption in the human relations movement in business management circles of some years ago which assumed that the more persons who are involved in the decision-making process the higher the ownership for the decisions. To some extent, that is an accurate assumption.

At the same time, there is nothing in the biblical material which suggests: "Be ye, therefore, on a committee—for great will be your reward in heaven." Indeed, a person can participate in a specific, concrete missional objective of the local congregation, be active in the corporate worship life of the community of faith, and belong to a significant relational group without belonging to a committee. And that person will have a higher sense of ownership for the life and mission of that church than the person who primarily sees church life in relation to being on a committee.

Again, in starting new congregations we need more missionaries and fewer professional ministers. We need to advance the training persons receive in seminaries across North America. One proposal for advancing that training in The United Methodist Church is to develop the ministerial educational program in such a way that seminaries receive funds from the apportionment on the basis of the number of students in the seminary and on the number of faculty who have had substantial experience as ministers in local congregations. Currently, the formula is based primarily on the number of students a seminary has.

There is a high percentage of faculty in medical schools who practice medicine day-by-day, week-by-week as physicians, even as they are engaged in major research and teaching responsibilities in the medical school. We need more faculty in seminaries who are engaged day-by-day, week-by-week as practicing missionaries in local congregations and communities, even as they are engaged in research and teaching on seminary faculties. This advance in training will deliver to our churches persons who are more likely to be competent, compassionate, committed, and courageous missionaries.

The second proposal that will enable us to have missionaries more fully involved in the life and mission of our congregations is to advance the tenure of a pastor to seven years. There are two reasons for this. First, a pastor is more likely to advance his or her competencies as a missionary and as a minister if given the chance to live with both the mistakes and successes in a given local congregation. It has been said that a certain pastor was in the ministry for twenty years, and someone responded, "No, he has really been in the ministry four years; he's simply done it five different places." There is some evidence to suggest that the most productive years of a pastor's local appointment begin around year five, six, or seven. We need to move toward longer tenure of pastors in congregations.

The second reason for moving toward longer tenure has to do with the entry and exit phenomenon. If, during the course of the seven-year period, a pastoral appointment is changed once, we have a year of entry with the first pastor and a year of exit with that pastor. We have another year of entry with the second pastor and a year of exit with that pastor. In the course of a seven-year period, we have four years of entry and exit and three years of reasonably productive ministry. We need increasingly to move to a pattern where, in the course of a seven-year period, there is one year of entry and one year of exit and five years of productive service as a missionary and minister for that local congregation.

The third major proposal that will enable us to discover more missionaries and fewer professional ministers is to see that serving as a pastor in the 1980s is more like serving in a M.A.S.H. tent on the front lines than serving in a big city hospital. You all know M.A.S.H., the remarkable delivery of competent medical and health care in a tent near the front lines. To be sure, the M.A.S.H. team worked themselves beyond exhaustion. Certainly, there were moments of anger, shouting, and crying. Moreover, there were moments of hilarity, laughter, and craziness. But amidst it all, there was the devoted commitment to deliver the best medical and health care that could possibly be delivered on the front lines. It is that kind of proactive and intentional missionary movement which pastors in the 1980s need to discover. It is the central driving theme that will enable their lives to count.

We need more Pauline leaders and fewer Rogerian listeners. We need more ministers who are missionaries and fewer ministers who are counselors. This is not to depreciate the value of listening or counseling. It is to say that this is the season for missionaries and evangelists.

PRIORITIES AND STRENGTHS

Priorities and strengths give direction and power to our work. The promise of priorities is that they give power to planning. In congregational development, it is decisive to set forth strategic priorities which focus and energize our human and financial strengths toward significant missional accomplishments and results.

Priorities must be set first because they inform and shape the rest of our work. This is especially true of strategic priorities.

A long-standing principle in strategic planning is as follows: 20 percent of the activities yield 80 percent of the results; 80 percent of the activities yield 20 percent of the results. Strategic priorities are the two-out-of-ten things which substantially shape the future, direction, and destiny of a denomination. Of 10,000 new congregations we might start, let us start the 2,000 which will best advance God's mission.

Priorities make it possible for leaders to work smarter, not harder. Whenever leaders view priorities as "more work," they are not taking seriously the function of priorities. That is, strategic priorities are not simply "added on to" everything else the leaders of a denomination are already doing. Rather, strategic priorities give shape and direction to those things which continue to be done and those things which the leaders of the denomination cease doing. Strategic priorities have decisive consequences for what we do in our week-to-week work.

The sixth foundational principle for congregational development is to develop strategic priorities which build on our strengths rather than running to our weaknesses. To deny our strength is to deny God. God is the source of those strengths we have. To claim our strengths is to claim the moving, living activity of God in our lives leading and drawing us toward that future which we have been promised and which has been prepared for us.

Regrettably, much congregational development has been based on a preoccupation with weaknesses rather than claiming strengths. Too many new congregations focus on their shortcomings, failures, faults, weaknesses, and problems. Not enough new congregations are helped to focus on their strengths, their competencies, talents, and gifts for mission and service.

A new congregation will claim the strengths it has in place. It will expand some of these strengths as it looks to the coming three to five years, and five to seven years in its life together. And it will thoughtfully and wisely add future foundational strengths that are commensurate with strengths already well in place and build them.

Now, this approach is not potentiality thinking. It is not possibility thinking. It is not naive optimism. Rather, it is a simple, biblical understanding of new congregations. To claim our strengths is to claim God's action in who we are as a people of God. To claim our strengths is to discover those competencies we have, to be effectively involved in mission in our community and around the world. To focus on our weaknesses is to develop a maintenance mindset and a siege mentality. To focus on the things we do well is to enable us to develop a mission mentality in the world.

HOPE

Hope is stronger than memory. Long-range planning is responsibly hopeful. Effective congregational development builds on the God-given hope that is (1) responsible and realistic, (2) courageous and compassionate, and (3) prayerful and powerful. Congregational development takes seriously the open tomb and the risen Lord of the Easter faith.

To be sure, congregational development appropriately studies sociological and demographic trends. It is useful that we consider such data projections but it is vital that we not become slaves to them in our decisions. Some so-called trends are simply self-fulfilling prophecies; that is, they come true only because enough people believe they will come true. Hence, they behave, act, and make decisions in such a fashion that they contribute to the trend running its predicted course.

We must raise serious questions as to whether certain so-called trends should be allowed to come to pass. For example, it was once projected that a given county would likely lose population, jobs, and school funds over a ten-year period. Enough people, businesses, and teachers believed the projections so that a quiet exodus began— and the trend came to pass.

In another county, similar so-called projections were put forward.

A pastor, a businessman, and a community leader did not believe the future had to be that way. In a realistic, courageous, and prayerful fashion, they set out to change the projected future of their county. The struggle was, in fact, enormous. New industry did come. New school funds were developed. New jobs were created. New people did move in. Other people, planning to move, decided to stay. The quality of life in the county did improve.

It will not always happen this way. But Christians rely on God, not data projections. This reliance on God is responsible and realistic. We are called not to march blindly off the cliff, but to build a bridge to the other side.

This reliance on God—in hope—is courageous and compassionate, not timid and calculating. Too many people do congregational development in "safe, comfortable" ways. God does not call us to stay by the Red Sea. We are called to follow God into the wilderness. God calls us to a mission that invites us to be our most creative, constructive, and compassionate selves. We are called to be good shepherds in this world, and that means seeking out those who are lost.

This reliance on God is prayerful and powerful. It is strange that so many church development committees do not pray. They study statistics and charts. They draw up long lists of problems and needs. They fail to see the strengths that God has provided them. They discuss their options for the future more like amateur retailers than "called-of-God Christians." And they wonder why they fail!

Effective church development builds on a God-given hope that is prayerful and powerful. The church development committee needs to genuinely pray, "What is God calling us to do as the people of God?" And, though our vision may focus on the coming five-to-seven-to-ten years, our eyes look beyond these time horizons to all that God is preparing for us in the future yet to come. There is power in the steady, solid confidence of this vision.

Some churches, like some people, believe their best years are behind them. Effective, successful churches live in the confidence of God's promise that their best years are yet to come. "And He who sat upon the throne said, 'Behold, I make all things new' " (Rev. 21:5). Effectiveness, mission, research, resources, missionaries, priorities and strengths, and hope—these are the principles that are fundamental in congregational development.